GREEN TIMBER

GREEN TIMBER

ON THE FLOOD TIDE TO FORTUNE
IN THE GREAT NORTHWEST

Thomas Emerson Ripley

This book is a joint publication by
American West Publishing Company
and Washington State Historical Society

AMERICAN WEST PUBLISHING COMPANY

PALO ALTO / CALIFORNIA

*"I could do once more
with a taste of the
bubbling well of enthusiasm,
sweet and heady, on tap
for the young men and women
of a new town."*

INTRODUCTION

BY BRUCE LE ROY

Tacoma in 1890 must have been exciting to a young man fresh from Yale. Its selection as the western terminus of the Northern Pacific Railway in 1873 had pushed the town to commercial prominence, and not until the Klondike gold rush, twenty-five years later, did Seattle begin seriously to challenge Tacoma's supremacy. The city to which Thomas Emerson Ripley came in 1890 was prosperous and booming. Here was the pulsing heart of the timber empire of the Pacific Northwest. Foreign sails crowded her harbor. Great ships moored at the longest dock in the world to load logs hauled to tidewater. Cargoes of grain from eastern Washington, Idaho, and Oregon arrived by rail to be poured into the holds of ships from around the world.

An impressionist in prose, Tom Ripley captured the frontier flavor and heady contrasts of this booming little metropolis. The light, shadow, color, and movement of his writing suggest the methods that James McNeill Whistler used to portray scenes beside the Thames of Victorian England. Unfortunately, Ripley, himself a painter, left no known studies of Tacoma. His only surviving paintings were created on trips to Europe and California in later years. But the quality of these substantiates the impression that he always saw life through the eyes of a graphic artist; *Green Timber* makes this apparent.

A few people still living on Puget Sound remember Tom Ripley well. My favorite historian of early Tacoma, Miss Ruby Blackwell, now ninety-two, recalls vividly young Tom's first arrival on Commencement Bay. She remembers when the handsome young Ivy Leaguer first walked into "Blackwell's," at that time the finest hos-

11

telry on Puget Sound. The establishment was owned and managed by Miss Blackwell's father.

"He was quite a charming scalawag," she recalls with a twinkle. "I was of an age to be impressed. Quite a few young men from Yale came here in those days. Some came for adventure. Some came to make a quick fortune. Others came 'to the colonies' because their families kicked them out west in the hope that they might grow up a little. These were our 'remittance men,' who sometimes lived just on the monthly check received from the folks back east.

"Not that Tom Ripley was ever in that category! His brother was already established here, and Tom went right to work for Wheeler Osgood. What's more, he stayed with the firm, eventually becoming president of the company. But Tom had his looks and charm, and well he knew how to use them! I think he broke several hearts (not mine) when he went back east and returned with a new wife."

Thomas Emerson Ripley was born in Rutland, Vermont, on September 19, 1865. His father, William Y. W. Ripley, was a Union general during the Civil War, commanding one of Lincoln's favorite regiments, the First United States Sharpshooters. Wounded at the battle of Malvern Hill, where his horse was shot out from under him, he was awarded the Congressional Medal of Honor for heroism under fire.

Young Tom represented the eleventh generation of Ripleys in America. The family was identified for generations with the famed marble industry of Vermont. In a book of delightful reminiscences, called *A Vermont Boyhood,* the author foreshadowed the prose technique of *Green Timber.* He defined artistic consciousness as "the screen of memory — at once sharp, jiggly, confused — followed by a sudden click and darkness, a whirling kaleidoscope of dissolving views." The result, for Ripley, was a series of vivid pictures somewhat like the popular "panoramas" of the nineteenth century, which moved along a track, giving the audience the impression of actually traveling by train through New England hills and valleys, or, in another popular series, of voyaging down the St. Lawrence River while the scenery flowed past in ever-changing color and mood.

Among the many images on Ripley's "screen of memory" is a sketch in miniature of his tremendous father: "'Tom,' he once said to me, glass in hand as he poured his customary three fingers of whisky, 'there is just one man in ten thousand who can drink with impunity — and by Jove! I'm that man.'" Ripley added, "The prohibition movement was then in full tide, and Frances Willard was stirring the prohibition pudding and the hearts of mothers and wives. So — even that one strong man in ten thousand took his dram in the bathroom, as a concession to family prejudice."

General William characterized young Tom early in the game when he said of his three sons, "I have two workers and one fiddler." Tom admitted many years later that "only the fiddler remains to paint his picture." He carried the conviction to Tacoma where he once said, "My business friends call me a painter, while my painter friends call me a businessman." Despite the self-deprecation, typical of a New Englander, the author did save a major business venture from disaster and then made his way to the top of the corporate structure.

When we consider his family traditions, we go a long way toward assessing what impact the Puget Sound country must have had upon the young man from Yale. Ripley remembered how his grandfather had "sputtered about 'the smelly rabble' which invaded the White House at Andrew Jackson's inauguration." And how Uncle Cyrus had "zipped around" fashionable London in the company of Charles Francis Adams, the American ambassador. Once Cyrus's wife, Mary, wrote home that "Cyrus was invited to go with him [Adams] to the House of Commons where Mr. Disraeli is to bring his reform bill."

Then there was lovely Aunt Julia, half-Yankee, half-French, who had "sent out her out-pourings in prose and verse." Her home, "The Maples," was a rendezvous for New England's *literati,* and her admiring visitors included Emerson, Holmes, Whittier, and Whitman. Even Mark Twain made the pilgrimage early in his career. "The Maples" was a mysteriously fascinating destination for a small boy, too. Tom remembered the family anecdote his mother told one day as they made the trip in a spanking new carriage up the high hills to Aunt Julia's retreat. An elderly lady who had accompanied Mrs. Ripley on the journey up to "The Maples" was somewhat concerned on the way home down the steep hills about the horses' straining backward against the breeching to keep the carriage from running away. "I put my faith in the Lord," said the old lady; "I prayed to God till the breechin' bust — and then I jumped."

Family involvement with the great names of New England may not have been so influential for young Ripley as the exploits and derring-do of Uncle Charlie, his father's youngest brother. Charlie made a legendary trip to the Far West in the 1870's "to investigate the mining interests." The folks back home held that objective firmly in mind (Charlie might have found a mother lode), but the trip produced only stirring letters about Indian skirmishes with western settlers, a real stagecoach holdup, and cowboy life in Montana. Uncle Charlie's western odyssey set young Tom to dreaming in technicolor. The amazing thing is that such exposure to Uncle Charlie did not prevent Tom from following family tradition, going on to Phillips Andover, then to Yale, where he graduated with the class of 1888.

In 1889 Wheeler Osgood Company, manufacturers of "doors, sash, and millwork," was organized in Tacoma, and Tom's older brother, William Ripley, went west to become plant superintendent. At William's urging, Tom joined him the following year. With help from the beneficent General, Tom purchased a small interest in the company. His first title was "secretary," but his real job was with the sales department, where it was decided he could gain the widest experience.

Double disaster struck in 1893. William died suddenly, and Tom was burdened with greater responsibility. Then the terrible business panic of 1893 ensued. Markets collapsed, and business, particularly in the Northwest, was nearly paralyzed.

To help the foundering firm, Ripley traveled east in search of new markets for the firm's products. Eventually, he was successful, particularly in New England, where family connections helped. But, in 1902, Wheeler Osgood's main plant was destroyed by fire, Tom returned to Tacoma and assumed the company's first vice-presidency and the general managership. He rebuilt the plant, broadened the business, and eventually became president of a most prosperous company.

Some of the historical figures in *Green Timber* were the movers and shakers of early Tacoma. Among these was C. P. Ferry, the "Duke of Tacoma," a son-in-law of General Matthew Morton McCarver, father of the new city. Ferry tried to name the new community "Commencement City" when the plat was filed in 1869, but he was overruled by Phillip Ritz, who suggested the name "Tacoma," based upon the Indian name, *Tahoma*, after the great mountain nearby. (Incidentally, few pioneer Tacomans have ever really accepted the mountain's later name, "Rainier," arguing that the alien admiral whose name it bears today had no real connection with either the mountain or the Puget Sound country.)

Another Tacoman mentioned by Ripley was Allen Mason — *bon vivant*, real estate promoter, and civic developer. Mason had a habit of journeying to far climes. His unique way of life was marked with such picturesque gestures as sending his wife an Egyptian mummy to compensate for overstaying his leave in the Middle East. On that occasion, his wife issued an ultimatum, and upon his return the mummy joined the new Ferry Collection, a museum named after C. P. Ferry, who also traveled and collected unlikely items from all over the world.

Nelson Bennett was another member of Tacoma's early Establishment, whom Ripley knew well. Bennett founded Fairhaven, in northern Washington, and had interests in many of the financial ventures that helped to promote the growing city on Commencement Bay. An engineering and financial genius, who built railroads, owned the Tacoma Hotel, the Tacoma *Ledger*, and (in partnership with Allen Mason) laid out Tacoma's street railways, Bennett made two great fortunes — the first swept away by the panic of 1893.

When Tom Ripley first arrived in Tacoma, many vestiges of the earliest pioneering period remained. For instance, Chinook, the Indian trade jargon developed as a means of communication between Indian and white fur trader nearly two centuries ago, was still in use. Though efforts were being made to erase this practice from business conversations to protect the innocent newcomer, no one cooperated much. The story goes that a circuit judge who was holding court was importuned by the defense attorney: "Your Honor," said he, "will you please instruct the prosecuting attorney not to address his remarks to the jury in a mixture of Chinook? They don't know what he's saying about my client."

"Absolutely right," intoned His Honor. "The prosecuting attorney will refrain from using Chinook when he addresses the Court. And, from now on, there will be no more *cultus wawa* in this courtroom!"

We are fortunate that Tom Ripley's family was eager to share this regional classic with a wider public than had access to the limited edition of privately printed memoirs that appeared six years ago. Much credit is due to Mr. and Mrs. F. Barreda Sherman, Ripley's daughter and son-in-law, whose persistence has finally resulted in this beautiful publication. Now, for the first time, students of northwest history, forest history buffs, and all lovers of good stories will have the privilege of hearing a master *raconteur* who was also a fine social historian. Add the wonderful period photographs from the collections of the Washington State Historical Society to the stories, and you have a book to be treasured.

Washington State Historical Society
Tacoma, July, 1968

GREEN TIMBER

PROLOGUE

"Within me, zones, cataracts, forests, volcanoes, groups." Walt Whitman said that, and as I look back to my youth on Puget Sound in those days of the early nineties, I have within me a whole Hollywood montage whirling across my memory in utter confusion, its parts whizzing by so fast that, try as I may, I can't put them in their proper order ....

On Tacoma's Pacific Avenue, the pounding of hammers and the screech of saws make exhilarating music. The groves, which yesterday were God's first temples, are being shaped into uncouth, false-fronted temples of whisky and provender. The real estate salesman, a roll of blueprints under his arm, joins his loud prophecies of easy money to the clatter of hammer and saw. Mud squirts up through the cracks of the loosely-planked roadway as horse-drawn loads of green lumber rattle down the street. Here and there, the tap of trowel handle on scarcely dried brick gives promise of solidity and permanence. The chief preoccupation, however, is quick shelter from the "liquid sunshine" of Puget Sound.

East and West! The twain are meeting in Tacoma; meeting in the common purpose to build an enduring city overnight, to gather in the profits of overnight turnover of corner lots. Chinese, still wearing pigtails, meet Philadelphians; Japanese, wearing "the more seemly derby, two sizes too large," meet Bostonians; native sons of California meet Down-Easters from the State o' Maine, asking, "What was your name back East?" Lumberjacks of the Saginaw, fresh from the skid roads and stepping high, meet Siwash Indians from their camp on the mud flats below the bluff.

The Northern Pacific is coming, snaking across the continent to terminus at the City of Destiny, the harbor of progress, the tree-studded land of plenty. And the Tacoma Ledger has broken into song:

> Move grandly on, thou car of fate,
> Deep freighted with a rich estate.
> Tacoma's dealers need not fear;
> The land is here — it is all here!

CHAPTER I

I WAS GRADUATED AT YALE — a much easier job then than it is now. I had completed my four years' course in glee club yodelling, guitar-playing, tap dancing, and other branches of the fine arts. The high school in Vermont had done the spadework of my education, thus putting the period to my Vermont boyhood. Andover, under Doctor Bancroft, had boosted me into Yale with two more conditions than the rubrics allowed; and in New Haven I had learned and practiced the gentle art of getting by. I was completely equipped for what President Timothy Dwight, in his baccalaureate sermon, called the Battle of Life. And if some serious-minded fellow doubts the value of that equipment, I am prepared to argue the question with him.

I took a train for Springfield, changed from one smelly day coach to another for Bellows Falls where — as did all travelers — I ate a fried pie and changed again into a smaller car for Rutland. Before the days of motors you couldn't get anywhere in Vermont *from* any-where without at least two changes. That's what made Vermont such a nice place in which to live.

In Rutland I emerged on Merchant's Row with my guitar, a suit-case stuffed with a month's unwashed laundry, my person clad in a complete outfit of what, in the language of *Town Topics*, the well dressed man should wear: a bobby-tailed cutaway, opened well in front to disclose a white waistcoat; trousers of a peachy hue, creased gracefully over toothpick patent-leather shoes and a baby blue tie fastened with my Scroll and Key pin. I carried a Malacca stick, over the head of which was folded a pair of immaculate dogskin gloves.

I surveyed sleepy Merchant's Row with an amused but, withal, a tolerant air. Peter, Rutland's one hack driver, waved an airy wel-come from the box of Rutland's one hack.

The General, my father, took one look — and it was a serious one. "What do you propose to do now?" he asked.

Truthfully I answered, "I don't know."

"Nobody is going to hire you for your fragrance," he said.

23

I doubted that but I didn't voice my doubts. I listened with the deference one always accorded the General.

"Get some overalls," he said. "I've arranged a job for you in the Howe Scale Works. You are to get a dollar a day — if you can hold the job. You start tomorrow."

It wasn't so bad throughout the green summer and the crimson and gold autumn months: getting up at five-thirty, wolfing a breakfast of coffee and sinkers at the Depot Restaurant, and hustling into jumper and denim pants as the whistle blew at seven. The ten-hour day was pretty long, but one could always beguile the time by bedeviling the foreman a bit and by frequent—and wholly unnecessary — trips to the toilet where one could read a month-old newspaper. But when the alarm clock sounded on dark, sleety winter mornings, it was not so good.

"Life is real — life is earnest," quoted Father. It *was*.

During the winter the musical name of Tacoma began to filter from the great western world to our sequestered little Vermont backwater. At first it sounded like the name of some new and delectable kind of canned goods, but the drumming guns of advertising soon cleared away the mystery and thereafter we had no doubts. Tacoma! A new city, carved out of the primeval forest, dipping its feet into the waters of Puget Sound!

A copy of a Sunday school paper that fell into our hands contained the invitation of Allen C. Mason to share the wealth of the new metropolis. I think it mentioned "Mount Tacoma, lifting its snow-clad summit fourteen thousand four hundred and forty-four feet into the clouds." Anyway, the phrase is indelibly etched on my memory.

The advertisement offered a twenty-five-foot lot in Mason's Addition for three hundred dollars. Further, it agreed that if the purchaser was not satisfied with his bargain after three years, Mr. Mason would buy the lot back at the purchase price plus interest at nine percent, compounded semiannually.

"Gosh!" said Harry Clement, the capitalist. "What more do you want?" Harry and his sister Charlotte had three hundred dollars in the savings bank. They pooled their resources and plunged. I didn't have three hundred dollars, but as I was engaged to Charlotte, I took a somewhat more than vicarious interest in her ownership of a home-site in the very farthest corner of the country. I did a lot of watchful waiting, rising to the bait, drawing off again, and rising to have an-

other look. I dreamed of salmon so thick that they crowded themselves out on the shores of Commencement Bay: the advertisement
said they did. I dreamed of sailboats, of virgin timber, of quick and
easy money that multiplied while you sailed and fished.

Always in the background was "majestic Mount Tacoma" rising
fourteen thousand four hundred and forty-four feet (we never
omitted the odd feet), feeding its living waters into the fertile valleys . . . The last frontier! . . . A young man's country! "Strong, silent
men under pressure of sail and steam!"

> The silence — the gloom,
> The glory of God — the room!

The phrases unrolled across my vision as on a ticker tape, while I
killed time at my bench at the scale works.

"Last chance — last chance!" sang the advertisements. "Hurry —
hurry!" before all those choice lots are gobbled up by the early birds.
There's gold in them thar hills — gold to be dug out by the simple
expedient of a down payment on a piece of ground and a quick sale
of the equity to the chap who comes in on tomorrow's boat.

> No need of miner's pan and pick;
> A fountain pen would do the trick.

From infection, through inflammation, to a full-scale epidemic, the
contagion spread. Harry Clement went first to take a job as greaser
for locomotives for the Northern Pacific, if and when its rails reached
Tacoma. The skeptical General, his lips uttering contempt for "all
this damned yap," his heart — confided to his fishing diary — stirred
with its inherited instinct to breach the Vermont corral, went along
with my big brother Will to spy out the land, crazy to see one of his
blood standing with the earth's adventurers.

And, less a hint than a command, he told me to bring a backload
of young elm trees to plant in front of Will's Tacoma home and a
collection of shoots from the "whistle tree," which, so long before,
had grown from Will's little-boy willow whistle at the back of the
white house in Rutland. He thought that a bit of Vermont foliage
transplanted from about Vermont's marble sidewalks wouldn't mar
the beauty of Tacoma's plank walks, beside which no deciduous leaf

had yet dared to show its green head.

But Father's telegram contained no word about Charlotte, who had long clung to her belief in me while her patience, I feared, might be wearing thin. Didn't Charlotte already own one of Allen C. Mason's three hundred dollar lots? Capital enough, we thought, for any pioneer. I composed a telegram. I used up a score of Western Union blanks trying to convey, in the ten words allowed before the advent of night messages, all the welling emotions of the past year of waiting. The best I could do was:

> WILL COME AT ONCE WAIT YOUR APPROVAL MARRY
> CHARLOTTE FIRST

I know now how great was the wrench to Father's sentimental heart, overlaid as it was with Vermont caution. He wired back:

> EARN BED AND BOARD FIRST THEN YOU CAN EARN
> CHARLOTTE

That postponed the question of matrimony. One didn't argue with Father. We settled upon six months as ample time in which to earn bed and board, and said goodbye.

"I have three sons," Father repeated. "Two workers and one fiddler." The older worker was shepherded off to seek his fortune; the younger worker was installed behind the black walnut counter of the Rutland County National Bank; the fiddler was doing his ten-hour shift in overalls and cap — the cap, be it said, set at a cock-o-hoop angle, the jumper concealing a heart which beat a tattoo for assembly in Tacoma.

In Tacoma Father became mildly infected with the virus which the new country supplied in such powerful doses. He did a lot of pretending to a tolerant skepticism but his creative urge was strong. An individualist was Father, and a rugged one at that. His ruggedness became strength when it came to giving a less lucky fellow a leg up, but he asked no man's help as he shouldered his own burdens. Now he nourished the idea of his sons carving out a home in the wilderness. At the back of his thought was the hope that he might lure his fiddler son from the degenerating influence of the arts he had acquired at Yale. He telegraphed me to come, the telegram containing a veiled hint that the guitar would be better left at home.

26

And so Allen C. Mason's little candle had thrown its beam across a continent. I promptly lighted my candle from his, and chose the Canadian Pacific as the most exciting haul for my long trek.

The Canadian Pacific Railroad was very new then. The golden spike connecting the East with the West had been driven but a short while before, and mine was one of the very earliest of the passenger trains to take the chance of disaster. It took a good seven days to reach Vancouver — seven days of high adventure. The train rambled across the prairies at a careful pace, stopping a whole day at Winnipeg, where British caution and British leisure insisted on a long rest and a thorough overhauling of its running gear. It paused at Regina, and my spine squiggled at sight of a Canadian mountie in scarlet tunic, rakish hat, and spurred boots. "Duke's son, earl's son?" Baronet's son anyway. "All gentlemen rankers," a chap told me. I asked the mountie but he didn't seem to know about that.

Moosejaw! "The place-where-the-white-man-mended-his-cart-with-a-moose-jawbone." Indians squatting on the platform! I looked for a pretty, dusky Indian maiden. The one I saw wasn't very pretty, but I pointed my camera at her anyway. She threatened me with a piece of scantling and demanded two bits. Medicine Hat, where a pillar of flame shot upward from the prairie. "It's this 'ere natural gas," said the brakeman. "They light it up when the train goes by so's the passengers kin see it. No, they don't use it — too busy sellin' real estate."

Beyond Calgary, the train climbed up, left the blossoming prairie, and plunged into the gap amid the snows of May. It crept through Banff and on down through the Kicking Horse Pass, its whistle screeching for the open switch, its brakes shooting a shower of sparks, an anxious brakeman hanging off the steps of the rear coach watching the fireworks. It disputed passage with the roaring Fraser and the Thompson. I hung, popeyed, to the rail of the rear platform all the way to Vancouver.

There I got a foothold on the deck of the steamer *Queen* bound down-sound for Tacoma.

The ship docked at Port Townsend, but not at Everett; there wasn't any Everett. She didn't stop at Fairhaven, now a part of Bellingham; Fairhaven existed only on blueprints. She may have hesitated at Seattle — I don't remember. I was a Tacoman and, if she did nose into the dock at Seattle, I am sure I looked the other way as we touched that upstart village whose mistaken inhabitants were pretending a rivalry with the City of Destiny, thirty miles to the south.

I stood at the bow as the *Queen* churned her way past Vashon Island, all misty blue and bronze green, and Brown's Point, with its timber as yet untouched by the ax. We cut a wide circle about Commencement Bay. I saw the smoking waste pile of the Old Tacoma Mill through a forest of windjammers' spars, smelt the bitter black smoke of the St. Paul and Tacoma mill stacks, and the weather being kind, glimpsed "majestic Mount Tacoma" between curtains of cloud.

CHAPTER II

BROTHER WILL had lost no time. He had taken a flyer in real estate. He had bought two lots, each twenty-five feet wide, on North E Street on the edge of, if not in the dead center of, Nob Hill. And so confident was Will that the town would promptly build itself up solid, like New York, that he had built his house on one twenty-five foot lot against the time when the next ambitious fellow wanted shelter among the homes of the wealthy. The house looked like a fancy Mississippi River boat, long, low and rakish, plowing its way into a haven of prosperity, jam-packed with recently born passengers. Will's windows let in light from fore and aft, the beam lights so arranged that they could be closed when the newcomer should build smack up against him. I bunked down on the starboard transom, a hard and narrow couch in what would have been the saloon if the house was ever launched.

It was a wooden city that I looked out upon the next morning, with the forest which gave it birth still keeping its inviolate secrets, its greenery pressing in upon it from all sides, but with no blade of green within. The wooden streets were flanked by sidewalks built up on wooden stilts on the downhill side. The houses on the upside were reached by steps, so many and so steep that going home seemed hardly worth the effort. The foundations were of wood — cedar, durable through the ages — supporting the riot of wooden shingles, wooden rustic, and more than seven wooden gables.

The plank road stretched its clattering way up St. Helen's Avenue, reaching out over the wooded hills, dropping down, passing on its way within sight of "the oldest ball tower in the world." Tiny St. Peter's church, rough carpentered, showing the "loving marks of the hammer" all over it, stood among its shack brethren smack up against Tacoma's last remnant of God's first temples — a mammoth fir trunk that formed the tower for the clanging bell on its sawed-off top. Its pride of hoary antiquity was justified. If I could have counted the ring growth record of its years, I would have found that the living

29

bell tower had stood there, defying the buffetings of Puget Sound storms, long before Gray wrote of "Ye distant spires," before the Meeting House of Hingham called my tight-lipped ancestors to prayer, perhaps before the devoted monks placed the stones of Glastonbury Abbey.

Less than a quarter of a century before, with many a "Yo-ho-ho" — and surely a bottle of rum — the bell had been hoisted to the sawed-off top by the crew and tackle of a sailing ship that lay at anchor off Old Tacoma. It was a roistering crew which first heard its sobering tones before the ivy, rioting to the top, had almost choked the voice of the bell. I added my share to our town pride in the tower that God had wrought long before the white men came. Surely, I thought, God comes to listen when Chaplain Stubbs of the Sailors' Mission prays in that green-clad chapel. I hadn't yet heard how Deacon Atkinson, the "swearing deacon," used to stick his head in turn into each of the clustering saloons of Old Town and yell "I want every damned man of you to come to church, and every damned man will put four bits into the plate"; nor how the sailors and loggers first called time on their fights and came, to catch their breath for the next bout. For a moment Stoke Poges came to mind. I wondered what sort of elegy might have been written on this country churchyard. It wouldn't bear thinking of.

Contemplation was punctured by the staccato of the shingle saws down by the water, where big Hanson had planted his mill on Job Carr's claim. I footed it down the plank sidewalk, heartbeats responding to the heartbeats of the monster. I thought of Rube Ranger's toy sawmill at Mill Village, up the mountainside from Rutland: Rube, swearing Vermont oaths, manhandling the little logs with his peavey; Rube cutting the baby things into baby sticks; piling the picayune rungs for Vermont chair factories; Rube calculating Vermont profits while he acted as his own head sawyer, yard foreman, and roustabout. And suddenly, like a fade-out on a movie screen, the play mill was lost to memory, blocked out by this voracious Gargantua, swallowing the growth of centuries at a gulp and spewing out the digested product. A Vermont guitar player stood face to face with a man-sized job. Would he ever be able to horn into this game with the big boys? His shirt buttons strained with his chest expansion.

The head sawyer was a chesty boy. He had a more valid right to be chesty, for power was unloosed at the touch of his hand. In the

30

way of all head sawyers, he affected indifference to the admiration of the tenderfoot, but he looked for it nonetheless. He squinted my way as the forty-two-foot log, six feet in diameter, obeyed his careless twist of the wrist and groaned its captive way up on the bull chain. A touch of another lever and the "steam nigger," a wicked-looking monster with teeth, turned the log best side out, patted it, coaxed it, and then, with a mighty *wham!* boosted it to its doom on the carriage. The chockers, legs apart against the speed of the carriage, drove their wedges into the log and braced themselves.

"Speed 'er up," shouted the foreman, and *bang* went the giant on the carriages, hitting the whirring saw which whined its way into the very midriff. Cants tumbled into the transfer chains and traveled to re-saw and edger. What did it matter that boards and plank emerged on the rollers a bit uncertain as to thickness and wavy as to surface?

"Fer th' Damfino saloon," said the foreman. "An' God! but they're hollerin' fer 'em."

Ike Striker, the architect and contractor of the Damfino, stood at the tail of the mill. "Anyway," he said, "it'll make the front look more rustic-like."

A conveyer chain, loaded to the frayed edges of the guards, carried its load of perfectly sound lumber to the burner and added its stream to the ever-mounting pile of burning wealth. The gray pile spread its pall of smoke heavenward to proclaim riches so inexhaustible that it mattered not that a good half went on the chains to the ghost mountain of ashes.

"Vertical stuff is what we want. Send the slash grain to the burner. There's plenty more. The best is none too good for me."

The impassive head sawyer hit up the pace for the sweating men at the tail of the mill. Planks for roadway and sidewalk, mud sills for shack foundations, siding, shiplap, and lath tumbled out at the rear to the ever-waiting line of wagons standing in the mud outside.

Dodging flying timbers, I followed along from head saw edger to automatic trim saw, finally to the tail of the mill. Ike Striker's load was making up. Ike was a raffish-looking cuss in his big hat, mackinaw coat, and high boots. He wasn't the *Virginian* sort of pioneer I had read about, and he didn't look like a good man to tangle with. He looked at me with a nice blend of contempt for my verdancy and curiosity as to my origins. He gnawed a sizable chew from his plug and spoke, his voice coming from the corner of his drooping mouth with no visible labial movement, like that of a ventriloquist.

"Stranger in town?"

"No. I belong here."

"Well, wouldn't that jar yuh! Reg'lar ol' mossback, ain't yuh? What's your line? Real estate?"

"No, not yet."

"Eastern money? Bankin' mebbe?"

"No. I don't think so."

"You don't look like a good barkeep, now; how about lumberin'?"

Ike said he was a *con*tractor. What this town needed, he said, was some more sawmills. I thought so, too. He said he was going to build a whole street full of darn nice houses up in the north end and he couldn't get lumber fast enough nor cheap enough. Now if I would build a new mill, I could run 'er night and day and make a barrel o' money. "Easy," he said. "Nothin' to it."

His load made up, Ike climbed aboard. "Want a ride?" he asked.

"Which way are you going?"

"Goin' *my* way," said Ike. "Foller me an' you'll wear diamonds."

I climbed over the wheel. Ike gathered up the ribbons. "Giddap, horses," he said.

As we jolted over the planks, Ike told me all about the future of the lumber business. That was the first time I had heard the words and music, but in the years to come I was to hear them repeated and again repeated, till I knew the libretto by heart. It was like a West Coast psalm, sung at matins and evensong. And boy! Did I believe it! It went like this:

"We got th' only big chunk o' standin' timber left in the world. White pine all cut off back there in Wisconsin an' them states. They've wasted their substance back there, as th' sayin' goes. Now they gotta come to us an' we got th' stuff to give 'em."

Then Ike got lyrical: "An' there's China with her teemin' millions. An' there's them Japs, livin' in paper houses, they tell me."

By the time we had topped the rise, and Ike eased on the brakes for the downgrade into the new Tacoma, Ike's rhetoric, spiced with tobacco juice, had ceased to sound funny. It began to sound like the seasoned judgment of a man of experience. I needed a voice of experience and began to dream dreams of a big, clattering sawmill, which would obey the touch of my masterful hand.

"Tacoma! Tacoma! Aurora! Aurora!"

The Wheeler Osgood Company, Ripley's introduction to the go-ahead world of western enterprise (left foreground, above), is dwarfed by the dim and impressive sweep of "Majestic Mount Tacoma"—which Tacoma's arch-rival Seattle had christened Mount Rainier.

"Seattle indeed! Trying to tag our mountain with the name of an unknown admiral—a British one at that. The curse of the mountain, we called that. No, better stick to Tacoma; and, all together now, Boost — don't knock." Below, an overview showing construction of the Tacoma Avenue Bridge over Old Woman's Gulch.

"Confidence in the future found expression in architecture— the more confidence, the more spindles, jig-sawed brackets, and band-sawed cresting atop the roof. . . . The seats of the mighty were marked by round towers at the corners, topped by minarets that looked like candle extinguishers. . . . The word of ambition was spindles."

"We got the only big chunk o' standin' timber left in the world," Ike Striker said. "White pine all cut off back in Wisconsin an' them states. They've wasted their substance back there, as the sayin' goes. Now they gotta come to us an' we got the stuff to give 'em." Above and below, the ships and mills of Tacoma prepare to export the substance of the Pacific Northwest.

"*The Northern Pacific people had selected a lovely headland overlooking the bay as the site of the long promised tourist hotel. Above the greenery of Old Woman's Gulch, the stupendous new hotel was to make the Frontenac in Quebec and the Canadian Pacific Hotel in Banff blush for their modest proportions.... Here was a veritable chateau of the Loire.*"

CHAPTER III

MEMORIES OF THOSE FIRST turbulent years in Tacoma are nebulous and confused, lacking, as they are, the strands of great national events to bind them together. Tacoma was far removed from the conflict of forces, the outcome of which was to mold our destinies in ways wholly unconventional to the eyes of a good Vermont Republican. While we pursued our rowdy way, I was content to leave it to the president to protect us against the dread attacks of the Farmers' Alliance and the sinister economic theories of the Populists. The Populists were making a lot of noise expounding their own notions of freedom. Oh, yes, I heard the echoes, but they mostly came from east of the Cascades and I thought them funny. The president, with the assistance of Czar Reed, Boss Platt, and Matt Quay, could be depended upon.

Only a picture, untidy and exultant, remains — a picture of a city bellying out from its mud-and-muddle diapers. We were the terminus. Just what this magic word implied to the eager crowd it would be hard to say. Would the Northern Pacific give those other towns the complete go-by, not even hesitating at upstart villages like Seattle as they puffed their way past? Probably.

Boston and Philadelphia had laid the cultural foundations of our town; New York had laid the financial cornerstone; the fluid Middle West had contributed her corn-fed, husky strength to the structure. All three gaily slapped shingle, and mortgage onto new houses. Confidence in the future found expression in architecture — the more confidence, the more spindles, jigsawed brackets, and band-sawed cresting atop the roof. The humbler requirements were met by Gothic windows, "art glass" transoms, and fancy butted shingles. The bastions of the mighty were marked by round towers at the corners, topped by minarets that looked like candle extinguishers. Nob Hill and the "nigger tract" alike painted their houses a variegated brown up to the belt course and finished up above with various liver shades of red. The refinements of ornamentation didn't stop with the outside. No, sir! Heavily carved newel posts greeted the eye through the bevel glass of the front door, and from the hall one passed from the drawing room to library between columns made in imitation of twisted rope, under a chaste design of turned spindles, which formed the inevitable grille. The word of ambition was "spindles."

As we walked downtown over the creaking plank sidewalks, Father unfolded his plans. "There are two men here who are organizing a company to make doors and windows — and spindles, Mr. Wheeler and Mr. Osgood. These two men are *terribly in earnest.* I have arranged to buy stock in their company for you and Will. Young George Osgood is the bookkeeper." My brother Will, already six weeks on location, listened. Will looked terribly in earnest, too. I flexed my mandibles, trying to look terribly in earnest like the rest. "Yes, sir," I said.

As we came down toward Ninth Street a flock of sheep bleated and blatted in front of Abe Gross's new store, advertising Abe's new stock of woolen goods. Abe was conducting a grand opening of "the only brick store in town," with a clock in the tower "costing eight hundred dollars." Up the street marched the Tacoma Silver Cornet Band, its tooting instruments blaring "Tacoma, Pride of the West." Behind the band came Mason's Zouaves in blue monkey jackets and baggy red pants, cutting pinwheels and other funny evolutions as they marched, the commander, Ned Parsons, issuing his orders by mysterious signals with his sword.

Behind the Zouaves a line of carriages carried the gentlemen and lady clerks from the old frame store to the new brick one. The gentlemen wore silk hats and ascot ties, and the girls were happy in new spring bonnets and bustles, all from Abe's stock.

"The only brick store in town!" The carriages rolled up to the entrance, where the silk hats and spring bonnets alighted and entered, received by Abe himself, who, smiling impartially upon all, acted the part of his own doorman. The crowd surged in, each hotfooting it, panting to be the first of Abe's customers. A triumphant and perspiring woman won the distinction of buying a paper of pins for which she paid twenty-five cents.

Father thought of Ben Burt's millinery store on Merchant's Row in Rutland. "Twenty-five cents for a paper of pins! Whew!" he said.

"But, sir, think of the freight," said Abe, who stood nearby rubbing his hands. "Think of the freight!" The phrase was the rubber stamp

34

of approval on all price gouges. In Tacoma, quarters were the common medium of exchange. Dimes and nickels were used by the thrifty but pennies were taboo. "When a country gets so goddamn mean that they use nickels and coppers, it's time for a he-man to move on." Father jingled his small change and thoughtfully transferred it to his hip pocket.

We walked down to the tide flats and footed it across the Wheeler Osgood waterway on two planks which teetered up and down as we straddled the crack between. We made our way to the board-and-batten office, where we found the ruthless, "terribly in earnest" pair in conference over the betterment of the means of salvation in the Sunday school and the raising of funds for construction of the Congregational Church. I had expected a pair of pirates, tough and hardboiled. I found two kindly gentlemen who had migrated by the usual route of the pioneers from New England, by way of Iowa. Like most migratory New Englanders, they had cropped the lush grass of the Middle West till it grew short, and then moved on to the rich pastures of the Pacific slope. Dubuque and Des Moines had been their religion for a space. They had changed their faith, and now their spiritual and material souls were knit into the new heaven on Puget Sound, the means of faith concentrated in a sash and door factory, the hope of glory in the Congregational Church.

Young George Osgood sat on a high stool and extended the right hand of fellowship with a charming mixture of warmth and shyness. We took to each other at once.

Brother Will, with the technological knowledge gained through four years of grind at the Massachusetts Institute of Technology, had already become superintendent of the factory and was deep in the mystery of blind stop and parting bead, rail and muntin, bracket and spindle. I was given a catalogue of all the architectural monstrosities of the period. Harry Osgood was in the shipping room, busy with promises to importunate contractors, who stormed the office demanding a stream of millwork for their half-finished houses. It seemed that the new factory could never supply the wants of the growing town.

A gray-haired old chap sat in a corner, estimating costs, adding a liberal profit, and then, lest he had forgotten something, doubling his bid. "Here," he said to the waiting customer, "I've forgotten something. See that speck on the blueprint? I thought it was a fly speck,

35

and, by golly, it's a rosette worth five dollars. Gimme that estimate again. Ain't you got a detail o' that rosette? Well, rosettes is worth ten dollars."

"I heard you the first time," said the customer. "Five dollars."

"That's when you got a detail. When we got to make a detail it's ten dollars," said the old man. Ten dollars it was.

"Excellent estimator," said Mr. Wheeler. "Got his training in our factory in Dubuque."

"Next," said Mr. Evans.

Voices came through the open door of the shipping room, a strident woman's voice dominating the wisecracks of Harry Osgood, the shipping clerk.

"Red glass in my front door? Young man, what you tryin' to do to me? Thank God I'm a lady. I didn't live in no Mother Hubbard back east an' I ain't goin' to put on no Mother Hubbard now. Red glass in my front door! Young man, you must 'a' been brought up in Opera Alley. What I mean is, you take that red glass right out and put in something refined. Red glass, indeed!"

"My mistake," fluted Harry. "What you want is etched glass number 1467, with bird's nest pattern in the middle and marginal lights of — let's see — pink? No? 'Course not. Kind o' borders on the red, don't it? What you say to blue and yellow — with art glass transom? That'll look swell."

"Excellent salesman," murmured Mr. Wheeler. His one ear was deaf to the reference to Opera Alley, that byway of mystery where the ladies of the redlight lived, but his other ear was cocked to the sale of marginal light number 1728, topped off by art glass 522.

We crossed by an overhead bridge from office to factory and plunged into the maelstrom of whirring machinery, each machine contributing its buzz, wheeze or whine to the crescendo and diminuendo of a symphonic poem. A band saw twanged malevolently on fancy brackets and roof cresting. A jigsaw jigged its staccato tap dance. A row of lathes threw their chips and shavings from the heavy roughing chisels and then settled down and purred like 'cellos, as fancy and fancier spindles and porch columns emerged under the sharp gouges. The squash-squash of rubber mallets beat out the rhythm like percussion instruments as door smashers pounded odd bits of wood together into the semblance of doors. They tossed these to the clamp. Squeak and groan of compressed wood fiber and the door flew to the sander and, as if by magic, emerged from its maw smooth as silk from the spinning drums of sandpaper. Over all hung the incense of cedar, for the newfangled blower system had not yet been installed, and we breathed lungfuls of the sweet-smelling dust.

Upstairs, Otto, the carver, was at work on a monstrous oak newel post for the grand staircase of the new county courthouse. Otto's creative urge found vent in every form of ornate design that he could find in the Grinling Gibbons book. Cupids, sea shells, and garlands rioted all over the thing, and the nightmare was topped off by three grinning faces in high relief, a coy female in the center casting amorous looks at a happy satyr around the corner, while the third side was reserved for the sour face of the rejected lover.

"Kind o' — *you* know — kind o' *flirt*," said Otto.

"Excellent artist," said Mr. Wheeler; "trained in our Dubuque factory."

We turned to the engine room. Franklin held court there, the despot of the small power plant. "Eternal vigilance" was engraved on his scutcheon, and he repeated it like a battle cry, emphasizing it with a wave of his monkey wrench. Old John, the fireman, straightened his back from the fire door and said, "That's so." He held his job that way.

"Excellent engineer," said Mr. Wheeler; "learned his trade in Dubuque."

"Yes, sir," I said; "a man after my own heart." But, secretly, my heart was back upstairs with Otto. I have ever had a leaning toward the less useful and more fantastic attainments. "Eternal vigilance" was all right with me, but I hoped it might be confined to the engine room. The grist was far more interesting than the power behind the millstones. Like the miller who saw not all the water that turned his mill, I was content to let Franklin keep his "eternal vigilance" to his own evil-smelling kindom. (Once, in spite of "eternal vigilance," Franklin's engine stopped on a dead center. "What in tarnation made that engine quit?" roared Franklin. "I don't know," I said. "Fact is, I don't know what in tarnation makes it go.")

We took a peek into the drying kiln, Mr. Wheeler observing with satisfaction the gasp of the neophyte as the blast of superheated air rushed from the open door.

"'Airs from Heaven or blasts from Hell,'" quoted Mr. Osgood, who joined us here. He pulled his kind face into solemn lines.

37

"That's Scripture, Thomas," he said.

Mr. Wheeler grinned. "I know scripture, too," he said. " 'Seest thou a man diligent in his business? He shall stand before kings.' "

Back in the office, Life's Earnest Purpose began. I was handed one hundred crisp certificates of common stock of the Wheeler Osgood Company. Father produced a note to the Rutland County National Bank for ten thousand dollars. "Here's where you sign," he said. He endorsed the note, a precaution which seemed to me a wholly unnecessary affront, and I became a capitalist and an industrialist — the owner of an interest in the roaring cataract of West Coast development and, at the same time, a debtor of an exact equivalent to the deep-running, quiet waters of Vermont conservatism.

A meeting of the board of directors was held. I was elected to the board; and as my cocoon unwrapped itself, I emerged as secretary, and my name was printed among the officers listed on the ornate letterhead. On the quiet, I asked Mr. Wheeler what the duties of a secretary were. "Oh," said Mr. Wheeler, "I'll tend to all that." Which suited me perfectly.

We visited the Traders Bank where I was introduced to Mr. Fitch, its president. "Our new secretary," said Mr. Wheeler.

"Come out to grow up with the country?" boomed Mr. Fitch. "Splendid! Young man's country, you know."

Mr. Fitch was the authentic picture of the gentle, cultivated scholar from New York State, doing his feeble best to affect the manner of the hard-bitten westerner. It didn't fool a soul, least of all Father, the rock-ribbed Vermont banker. Father looked on in amazement at the graceful ease with which this new president of this new bank extended credit to all, like manna from heaven.

"Excellent bank," said Mr. Wheeler.

"Perhaps so — perhaps so," said Father.

But no doubts clouded my vision as we stepped out into Pacific Avenue. There I was interviewed by a reporter, to whom I expounded my views on The Building of a City. My welcome into the world of go-getters was hearty and warming to the cockles of the heart. Would I join the Commercial Club? Of course I would. I would join anything. The pin feathers of a fledgling industrialist pricked through my hide when Rit Wilkinson called me a "live wire." I loved it.

CHAPTER IV

THE PATTERN OF MY LIFE must have been traced for me by some unknown, easy-going ancestor who was not on the passenger list of grim-visaged early arrivals in Massachusetts. I am sure the lines of his face turned up rather than down. I cannot find him in my genealogy. Perhaps he was a thoroughly disreputable fellow; perhaps he was a man of God — with lapses. Whoever he was, and wherever his bones lie, I build a mental monument to his memory. The pattern that he traced was developed in the days of Yale when Father, battling, with hope deferred, clung desperately to the fancy that I was preparing for the awful struggle which, he was sure, awaited my generation.

"The time will come," he said, "when you will stand in your own doorway and defend your property with arms in your hands." Father never told me who it was that was going to attack me, but I believe he must have been thinking of Eugene V. Debs. Debs was the grand secretary of the Brotherhood of Locomotive Firemen. He was threatening the Bulwarks of our Liberty and, what came to the same thing, the Sanctity of Property. His very name, foreign-sounding as it was, was sinister.

Twice a year, once to give a fillip to the glad Christmas season and once to start me happily on the long summer vacation, Father called me into the library to examine my cash account with me and to urge me to a life of Earnest Endeavor. "Life is real! Life is earnest!" he repeated; and he rarely omitted a discouraging reference to the sweat of my brow. The auditing of the cash account was an unmixed horror, for his eye unerringly caught the signs of forced balances. With rapid pencil he computed the inordinate sums I had spent for postage stamps. "Tom," he said, "during the last term you have written six letters a day and ten on Sundays." Another ten minutes of silent figuring, and he produced a column of figures under the heading "lost under the horizontal bar." It was a thoroughly unhappy hour till Father relaxed with a grin and told me that I needed a little bit added to my allowance for the next year. I escaped in repentance and with stern resolution to go back to college and go in

39

for honors in political economy, history, and law. It sounded swell till I forgot just which honors I had elected.

Politically, my Vermont Republicanism found vent in the Blaine and Logan Battalion, in which I marched, clad in a tin helmet and a white cotton flannel coat, carrying a leaking torch and fighting the townies. James G. Blaine was the plumed knight of the party. Nobody seemed to care when he was charged with dishonesty. It made no dent on my social consciousness. Our democracy meant a glorious and enduring something which flowed from an unknown source like the waters of Otter Creek. We *had* it. It meant rights without price, which had sprung in ready-made armor, from the head of Jove. And, if my rights seemed to be infringed, I said, "There ought to be a law against *that*." I sat under Billy Sumner, learning and forgetting.

As for the life of toil and trouble which was said to lie ahead of me, I can't remember that I gave it much thought. Dreams? Yes. I dreamed of some shadowy eminence to which I would climb with no fixed purpose and no great effort. The way would open and I would march forward; and, in my dream march, I was always leading the parade, on horseback. In our senior year, we boys sat and carved our initials on Mrs. Moriarty's table tops; and, as we carved, Mrs. Moriarty's ale made our visions roseate. I had heard of the big fees that Stanford White drew down. Maybe I would be an architect — a great one. Another boy, who is now a rancher, elected the career of big business. A third chose the ministry and became a life insurance agent.

Alone among us, Gifford Pinchot knew what he wanted.

"I'm going to be a forester," he said. We laughed.

"What the hell's a forester?" we asked.

Gifford drew us a picture of the young knight of conservation, rambling through the forest and telling the lumber baron how to spare that tree and log it off at the same time by something he called "selective logging." Gifford alone among us had the Earnest Purpose. He did become not only a forester but *the* forester, and so earnest was he that he got himself fired by President Taft for too much competence.

Under compulsion I learned the little that the simple standard required. I experienced much that was not in the curriculum and a tiny residiuum remained with me as an alkaloid base upon which to build up a full life. Billy Phelps used to say, "The glory of the college is that it teaches nothing useful." In the light of my experience, I believe Billy Phelps was right. My schooling never taught me the manly frown, the squared jaw, the firm grip, which was to tackle life with its Challenging Interests and *handle* it — as advocated by the books which tell us how to develop character. My poor old character! It was born relaxed and has been practicing relaxation ever since.

And now, clad in this shining but frail armor, I stepped into the arena of business, where the game was played rough and tumble and no holds barred. I was the secretary of a company, with a salary, and a member of the board of directors. I got myself a motto to put on my desk. It read: DO IT NOW. The Vaughn and Morrill Book Shop catered to the motto-loving public of that day, and a counter full of mottos fairly screamed daily hints for daily needs; thoughts for the morning, telling one how to leap from bed with a glad shout, strengthening one's character and extending one's personality. They were so heartening that I bought two more: one exhorting me to DO THE HARD THING FIRST, and another that pleased me mightily, SO LIVE THAT YOU CAN LOOK ANY MAN IN THE FACE AND TELL HIM TO GO TO HELL.

A shiny new desk with mottos on it before me, a swivel chair under me, and I was ready to act my part, whatever it was.

Mr. Wheeler helped me. "Being a secretary isn't a full-time job," he said. "I think we would better give you another title. How'd you like to be the city salesman?"

I looked at my motto, DO THE HARD THING FIRST, and said I'd just love it.

True to their promise to make Tacoma journey's end for all travelers, the Northern Pacific people had selected a lovely headland overlooking the bay on which to build the long promised tourist hotel. Above the greenery of Old Woman's Gulch, its broad terraces and gardens rising tier upon tier from almost the water's edge to its towers and battlements, the stupendous new Tacoma Hotel was to make the Frontenac in Quebec and the Canadian Pacific Railroad Hotel in Banff blush for their modest proportions. Here was a job for a mill man to go after. If I could bag the contract for all that millwork, I would find justification for all my mottos. I tackled the hard thing first.

41

I found the contractor, Mr. Goss, amid a welter of yellow brick and steel girders. He looked tough and uncompromising. He called me "young feller": "Well, young feller, what do *you* want?"— like that.

"I am the secretary of the Wheeler Osgood Company," I said.

"Well, well," said Mr. Goss. "Who'd have thought it! Out o' school back east? Come out to grow up with the country?"

I tried again. "Mr. Goss," I said, "I want to sell you all the millwork for this hotel."

Goss laughed. "So that's it," he said. "Now you're learnin'. Come into the office."

He gave me a great roll of blueprints, sheets upon sheets of details, and a formidable set of specifications. I gathered them under my arm.

"Sharpen your pencil, now," said Goss.

In the office of Mr. Evans, the estimator, we unrolled the blueprints, which covered the desks and a good part of the floor. The architect's perspective showed a wide court in front, carriages rolling in, and dainty ladies in wide sleeves and bustles stepping out and into the spacious lounge. All the ladies showed dainty feet and a tiny bit of dainty ankle, surrounded by billowing lace petticoats. Ladies were dainty in those days or they just weren't ladies at all.

We pored over the blueprints with popping eyes and swelling hearts. Here was no five-thousand-dollar piffling residence, but a veritable chateau of the Loire Valley. We counted thousands of doors and windows, each with its pattern of French *croisée*. We measured baseboard and casing by the mile, and what pleased me most and made Otto fairly lick his chops, we foresaw a jungle of carving in rare and exotic woods. It was a riot of millwork. Creation in the busy factory, the profit motive going strong in the office.

CHAPTER V

LOOKING AT THE STATISTICS OF BUILDING — mounting population, real estate transfers — the story of the construction of Tacoma is not, I suppose, unlike that of many another American city that sprang up, miraculously, along the shining steel ribbons in the great era of railroad-building. If you stick your unsuspecting head into any chamber of commerce between Gopher Prairie and Detroit, you will get an earful and a pocketful of statistics, with pictures of airy skyscrapers puncturing the heavens in the search for desk room, while the expanse of prairie round about affords ample space to be reached afoot instead of in elevators. The pride in crowded population was not confined to Tacoma; it seems, unfortunately, to be inherent in the American mind.

But these statistical notes are as drab as stockmarket reports to one who owns no stocks. My interest in the building of our town lies not in these things. It lies in the many-faceted character of the men who came together west of the Cascades to help in its building. West of the Cascades was as innocent of the Ten Commandments as east of Suez. And wherever the Ten Commandments have been thrown into the discard, a vast array of various kinds of men will swarm.

And what a vast array of various kinds of men I have known! Trying to put their odd shapes together into a cohesive picture is like doing a jigsaw puzzle. A heap of shapes and colors lie before me. I hold one in my hand and find a hole where it fits. It is Stuart Rice, who, at the age of twenty-one, stood at a corner on Pacific Avenue, six-shooter in hand and resolution in heart, to keep what semblance of order he could amid the mob of self-styled vigilantes who drove the luckless Chinese out of town.

Racial intolerance was as strong in that small and isolated world as it is today in the larger world. In a still earlier day, the Chinese had been welcomed into the Northwest to do the heavier work when good Americans, eager for easy money, declined to bend their backs over pick and shovel. But when these selfsame Chinese displayed a willingness to work at less strenuous jobs, the cry of "Chinese cheap labor" rent the heavens.

Much was said about "dainty ladies' underwear puddled about in dirty suds," yet when the Tacoma Hotel installed a proper laundry, where the beruffled things could be handled with proper delicacy, the project folded up in the face of Oriental competition. John Chinaman, was, to be sure, a bit untidy and smelly in his wash house, but he was, on the whole, a peaceful, inoffensive sort of fellow. However, he was alien in speech and habit. It was enough. The scenery was set on this small stage for the brutal drama of persecution which we are witnessing on the larger world stage of today.

It is difficult after all these years to find a more valid basis for the anti-Chinese feeling that flared up and was fanned in the new community. Perhaps these English-speaking men with good English names had inherited something from godly New Englanders, one of whom said of a disease which decimated the Indians, "By this means, Christ made room for his children to plant." I question though whether Mike Ward gave much thought to the planting of Christ's vineyard or to any other planting. Mike Ward boasted that he could bite a piece out of a whisky glass and frequently performed that feat of gallantry whenever a willing showman could be found to buy the whisky. Mike shouted, "The Chinese must go," and the battle cry was taken up and roared lustily by the self-appointed Committee of Fifteen.

A new secret society under the hopeful name of "The New Era" had been born. Mike called it "The New Area." The Law and Order League took a hand and its meetings seem to have developed more skullduggery than was to be found among the unhappy Chinese. With meetings in halls and mobs milling about the streets, the fever spread. Rockets, torches, and red fire made the muddy streets luminous with one-hundred-per-cent American enthusiasm. Gallant women, ready as always to urge their menfolk on to dirty work, waved dainty handkerchiefs from the gallery as fiery speeches were made from the platform. From Seattle came a delegation to discuss mutual action. They were presented with a huge cake, baked by a woman whose "America for Americans" sentiments carried her as far as her cookery. It bore on its sugar-frosted top the legend THE CHINESE MUST GO. Secret committees with passwords — bloodcurdling oaths and cabalistic signs — laid the train, and at the prearranged signal, a blast from a steam whistle, the dirty work was done. The Chinese shacks were burned and the poor Celestials were driven to the outskirts of the town and left to wander in search of some place where the Christian spirit, of which they had been taught, was made more manifest.

The story makes a nasty chapter in the chronicles of Tacoma, and I tell it because the associational network of memory brings Stuart Rice into the picture. I like to think of Stuart, a gangling youth with a high heart, standing throughout that horrid day, his shooting iron in hand, saving many an Oriental exile from personal violence. Stuart lived to become "Uncle Studie" to the young things of a later day, and died rejoicing in the memories of the good days of the past, his eyes on the future of his beloved city. I once tried to make him tell me the story. "Don't remember a thing about it," he said.

The Reverend Mr. McFarland, doughty Scot by birth, sturdy American by choice, is part of the picture too. With the zeal of his hero, Calvin, he mounted his pulpit to cast his pearls of brotherhood before swine. The swine knew them not for pearls. One by one, the Chinese-haters got up and walked out on him. "Go! Go!" he shouted at their receding backs. "I will preach on till the benches are empty."

Informers visited his house to see if any Chinese were employed there, and his indignation rose to fighting heat. A militant Gideon, he stormed into the office of Captain Whyte of the National Guard. "Should a minister of the church of Christ carry arms?" he asked.

"A minister might be more comfortable with a revolver," said the captain.

"And may I have one?"

Whyte, as good a Scot as the minister himself, grinned, "You may have two," he said.

The reverend strapped two big ones about his gaunt waist and went about among his flock, preaching brotherhood to the men, calming the lady parishioners, the word of God made manifest in the two bulges under his long-tailed frock coat.

Far removed in doctrine, but bound in practice in close embrace, stands Father Peter Hylebos, defender of the Catholic faith. Father Hylebos was one of twins, born in Belgium. One twin was baptized Peter Francis, the other Francis Peter. With ten other children to identify, the parents lost count, and, like Buttercup, "mixed those babies up," with the result that Father Hylebos never did know which of the two names the Church had given him. It is characteristic of the fighting priest that he chose the name of the militant Peter rather than that of the gentle Francis.

All through that dismal day, Father Hylebos labored as a self-appointed deputy sheriff, a fighting man of God, counseling moderation where counsel would prevail, backing up his counsel with his big fist and his big bulk where they were needed. Like the wise chaplain, he stood quietly behind the scenes as long as possible, his shrewd mind prompting caution, cleverly distracting attention from the more riotous plans and saving the militants from bloody acts of lawlessness.

On his beat he found a vacant room into which he herded a gang of hotheads. He knew them all. His face wore the beatific smile of the village curé, while his big hand folded itself about the club which he carried. Inside, he told them of the law of the land and the law of the spirit, emphasizing the one with his big stick, the other with the upraised two fingers of priestly blessing. He wound up his five minutes of earnest discourse with, "And now you, Jim, Mike, Shorty, go about your business, and may the Grace of God be with you — and by the Eternal, you'll need it if you lay a violent finger on one of those yellow brothers of yours."

"Guess mebbe he's right, boss," said Jim.

Mike and Shorty agreed and filed out into the streets where, with hearts attuned to righteousness, they helped the evicted aliens to pack their duffel and depart in what peace there was to be found in Mike Ward's American world.

The spirit of Father Hylebos and Pastor McFarland tempered the violence of the mob like a blessing. A certain shamefaced gentleness suddenly became the fashion, and the hardboiled vied with each other in acts of loving kindness. Men who but an hour before had brandished clubs now turned to help the bewildered Chinese pack their pathetic belongings. From nowhere, a few wagons appeared in which the old folk and the children could ride, and storekeepers brought food for the journey.

It was almost like a procession of mercy that accompanied the evicted out to Lake View, there to await the freight train bound for Portland. When the train arrived, the good-natured conductor opened the empties, shouted, "Put 'em aboard — I'll haul 'em"; and the train of boxcars loaded to the guards with a sad lot of the homeless, rumbled on its way to Portland.

Actually, there was a majority of decent, kindly people in our town but they were helpless against the mob minority. A few spirited souls got their hackles up and resisted, like Ike Anderson, a cultivated representative of the "better class" who lifted his voice against the outrage where all could hear. Threatened with violence, he put two guards at his house and declared that he would give a prize of five hundred dollars each if they succeeded in wounding a raider, and a thousand if they managed to kill one.

And Mrs. Bowen, whose household was dominated by a Chinese servant, stood guard in her doorway, wielding her broom.

"Put him out," yelled the crowd.

"Put him out, nothing," yelled Mrs. Bowen, and she charged. She drove the invaders off and retired to extract the terrified Chinaman from under the kitchen sink.

The red fire burned itself out. "The shouting and the tumult died," and the good people of our town awoke from the nightmare with an uneasy sense that something intolerable had happened during a restless sleep. An amputation had been performed to ease the pain of an ingrowing toenail. The heroes who did the job felt no better. A federal grand jury was sitting, and the Committee of Fifteen began to hear such ominous words as "conspiracy to insurrection and riot," and "equal protection under the law." It was unpleasant talk for heroes, who sat about town in chastened knots pointing accusing fingers at each other. "The devil was sick—the devil a monk would be."

Arrests followed; after a short sojourn under guard in the courthouse, the ringleaders were taken for a ride to Portland for trial on the same rails that had carried the evicted Chinese there.

For years we could not lure the Chinese back to Tacoma, and they were sadly missed. "Portland all lite," they said. "Seattle pletty good; Tacoma *no* good."

One former Tacoma Chinese found a job in the Palace Hotel in San Francisco. Years later, my Scottish friend Aleck Thompson, coming from the elevator at an early hour, found him on his knees scrubbing the lobby floor. "Good mor-r-rning, Jawn," said Aleck. "Washee, washee?"

The Celestial rose, bowed like a Bayard, and riposted, in perfect Harvardese, "No, sir, you mistake; I am cleaning the floor. Hoot

47

mon! Eh, what, Tacoma?"

We lost many needed workmen, patient and skillful, and the temperamental Lena never quite filled the place in our kitchen of the impassive John. The day of "the ceaseless changing of help that hinders" dawned, and for years a popular device for the dining room read: "God bless our home — and damn the hired girl."

"Only a picture, untidy and exultant, remains—a picture of a city bellying out from its mud-and-muddle diapers."

George Francis Train, who attempted to go around the world in sixty days—from Tacoma to Tacoma, of course.

Stuart Rice, who stood on a street corner with gun in hand to protect the luckless Chinese from self-styled vigilantes.

The grim-jawed Committee of Fifteen, who rallied behind the cry of "The Chinese Must Go!" and during a day and night of violence managed to drive the Orientals out. "The good people of our town awoke from the nightmare with an uneasy sense that something intolerable had happened during a restless sleep."

On January 1, 1891, the Ledger *spread itself with jubilant editorials: "The remarkable figures in today's issue powerfully indicate the future of Tacoma. Not in the spirit of vain panegyric has it been styled the City of Destiny. Its rise to Metropolitan greatness and worldwide fame within a few brief years has been one of the romances of the nineteenth century."*

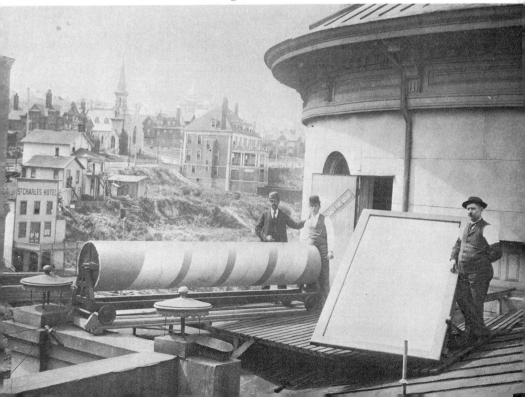

Blueprinting machinery at the Northern Pacific Headquarters required a commodity sometimes scarce in Tacoma—warm, bright, and continuous sunshine.

Staff and hangers-on of the Tacoma News, Pacific Avenue.

Faculty and students of the Tacoma Business College, Tacoma Avenue.

"Let ENERGY! AMBITION! and ENTERPRISE!
continue to give lustre to the City of Destiny."

The first brick building in Tacoma: Abe Gross's Dry Goods store, Pacific Avenue.

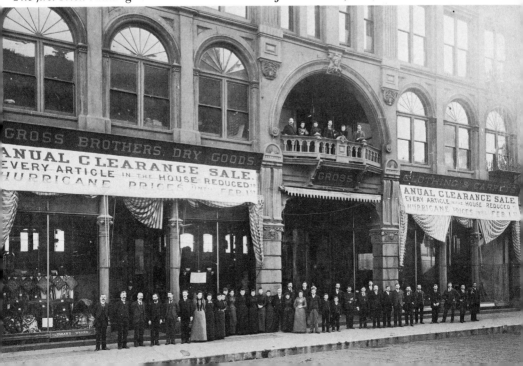

"I could do once more with a taste of the bubbling well of enthusiasm, sweet and heady, on tap for the young men and women of a new town." Above left, enthusiasm packs the house during an 1894 opening night at the Tacoma Theatre, Olaf Buel conducting. Constructed in 1891, the Tacoma Theatre replaced the Alpha Opera House, which had featured such luminaries as Modjeska, Henry Ward Beecher, and John L. Sullivan in its glory days. Commerce abhorring a vacuum, the Opera House promptly became a billiard parlor (left). Sic transit . . .

The intrepid Tacoma Wheelmen line up for a group picture in the days before "the old high wheeled bicycle with its solid rubber tires had given way to the high geared safety, rolling on rubber tires inflated with air, endangering life and property. . . . There was no limit to the marvels of the new age."

"The instinct for a decent and orderly life . . . very early sent up green shoots from the compost heap of heterogeneous material." At left, the Fern Hill Methodist Church Broom Brigade, a drill team that performed to raise money for pews and church furniture. Below, the Palmetto Social Circle lines up for decency's sake.

President Harrison made a tour of the West and stopped in Tacoma. "With a lively sense of benefits to come, we prepared to express our loyal gratitude in advance. Flags and bunting came out of storage, and triumphal arches were knocked together . . ."

"The President was driven through the less unpresentable streets that he might see and admire Great Babylon which we had builded. . . . With water running down our coat collars, we cheered ourselves hoarse, but the President promised us no new railroads, no river and harbor improvements—nothing. A wag went home and wrote for next morning's edition of the Ledger:

Tacoma's rain was falling fast,
As up Pacific Avenue passed
A hatband; underneath, a man
Who muttered, as he only can,
        'Drive faster!' "

"Ain't we got the longest wheat warehouse in the world? Ain't we got the Northern Pacific back of us? And the Tacoma Land Company? Ain't we got all the natural facilities for manufacturing in the world? We should worry."

CHAPTER VI

SO MANY LIVELY THINGS had happened in Tacoma before I ever saw the place, so much had already become legend, that I find it difficult to separate myself from all that had gone before. As I gave myself to the building of our town, so the town has built itself into a part of me, even the period that came before my time. I can't build a dam across the river of time, stopping its flow to say "lo here," and "lo there," for it is all of a piece. I say this to forestall some old-timer with a penchant for dates, who may say as he reads, "He's dreaming! He wasn't there!"

The impalpable part of me *was* there.

Henry Villard, Napoleon of Northern Pacific finance, had lost his fight to make Portland the terminus of the Northern Pacific Railroad. The good godfather Wright, president of the road, had switchbacked the rails over the hazardous route through the Cascades, direct to the New Jerusalem with its streets of gold.

"When you meet an obstacle," said Wright, "jump it."

"We are all floating on the flood tide to fortune," sang the Tacoma *Ledger*.

"Tacoma! Tacoma! Aurora! Aurora!"

"Portland! Portland! Tin can! Tin can!"

"Seattle! Seattle! Death rattle! Death rattle!" sang the victorious Tacomans.

Washington had but just emerged from the status of territory into full statehood. Why shouldn't Tacoma annex the whole kit an' bilin'? Hiaton, the old Indian, with a face like saddle leather, had said, "God gave the name Tacoma to the mountain." Why not extend His munificence to the whole state? Though the father of his country did deserve recognition, still, God and the snowcapped mountain had been here long before Washington's day and years before the British Admiral Rainier had clapped his name onto the mountain. Why not call the state "Tacoma"? Wouldn't those Seattle fellows gnash their impotent teeth when mail came addressed to:

Mr. J. Blighted Hope
Seattle
Tacoma?

Wouldn't they? Just?

The *Ledger,* with sail ever trimmed to a favoring wind, spread itself in its editorial column:

> Tacoma, beautiful, euphonious, appropriate. The greatest city in the East bears the name of the state in which it is situated. Let the greatest state in the Union bear the name of its greatest city.

"Good idea," said Ike Striker. "An' anyway, 'twon't be long before our city will reach clear up the Puyallup Valley right to Seattle's city limits."

"And there's Hawaii: those pearls of the South Seas," whose waters even now were being troubled by the annexation pudding stick.

"Why not let Hawaii in?" asked the *Ledger.* "The majority of Hawaiians of character and substance have longed for abolition of the monarchy. They look, with eagerness, with us, for the starry flag of protection and honor, floating over those lowly isles."

"Can't exactly take them into Tacoma," said Ike Striker, "but we can let 'em send their pineapples and sugar an' stuff through the longest wheat warehouse in the world."

With the completion of the switchback, the morning of life dawned again. Again the new town cut loose and capered. They hauled out the old gun — armament of a Russian gunboat which had come, "to boot," with the purchase of Alaska in 1867 — and they rammed it and they rammed it; and they fired it and they fired it till it was too hot to fire. Then they took a drink and they took another and they fired it again.

The switchback was built amid the snows of winter and rebuilt when the Chinook thaws undercut its bed. On a five-per-cent grade it climbed to the reverse horseshoe at the summit, and then it dropped on a grade steep enough to make your heart stand still. When the last spike was set. Mrs. Huson broke a bottle of champagne on its head. Her aim with the bottle was good, but when she swung for a mighty wham with the sledgehammer, she missed the spike. Bad omens never clouded the sun of those days. "A miss is as good as a mile," she said. She smiled prettily and yielded the sledge to Mr. Buckley, master of ceremonies, who rose gallantly to the occasion.

"And a smile is as good as a mile," he countered, as he drove the spike home.

So that no part of the business should be missed, each blow of the sledge was flashed by the tap of the telegraph operator from aloft to the world of the valley below.

Down in the town the streets bloomed with bunting. And what bunting Tacoma couldn't supply, Portland and Seattle sent, for "Trade follows the flag." Abe Gross, always at the forefront in matters of art, displayed over the door of his brick store an almost full-sized locomotive, puffing an inordinate lot of smoke from its insides. A triumphal arch spanned Pacific Avenue, extra warm in its welcome, for the sign painter, with reverse English, made it proclaim: HERE ARE OUR HEARTS WITH OUR HANDS IN THEM. Under Ike Anderson's direction, all hands turned to and built a huge pavilion on the bluff where Stadium High School now stands, on which to celebrate the arrival of the first train from "back east" direct to the City of Destiny. The pavilion, magnificent in proportions and somewhat flimsy in construction, held a good part of the whole population of rooters. Every available musical instrument in town was commandeered, and all who could sing a note — and a lot who couldn't — were herded to the platform where they waited, tense, for the pre-arranged signal, a blast from the locomotive whistle. The British man-o'-war, H. M. S. *Caroline*, lay at anchor in the bay, roaring her salute of twenty-one guns.

Down the grade came the wood-burning locomotive, its inverted cone of a smokestack puffing smoke rings. The whistle sounded. A hundred voices answered, struggling with the "Gloria" from Mozart's Twelfth Mass. As the tribute of the British guns died in echoes among the surrounding hills, prima donna Florence Molinelli, her white dress a bit bedraggled from the rain, stepped forward and recited as a graceful response to the British salute, the Declaration of Independence, and she put all she had into her defiance of King George and all succeeding royalties. The astonished British officers never batted an astonished eye as they pounded their applause with their scabbards on the shaking platform. The guns and music were followed by Major Henderson, "the drummer boy of Rappahannock," who gave an exhibition of his proficiency with the drumsticks.

51

The whoopee continued for three days, with Chinese lanterns illuminating the streets, fireworks by night and parades by day. Rival hose-cart companies raced through the streets, and prizes were given to those that could squirt the quickest and farthest. At each of the forty-odd saloons that lined Pacific Avenue, free drinks were handed out to the dazzled train crew of the first "through" train.

The élite (in those dark ages we didn't know the word "socialite") flocked in the evening from Nob Hill to the Tacoma Hotel, where, on the broad terrace overlooking the tidal flats, the Hawaiian band titillated the new society with strange and wanton tunes.

This great hotel (described, American fashion, as "the two-hundred-and-sixty-seven-thousand-dollar hotel"), had just been opened. Stanford White himself had planned it. "When you're getting an architect," said Mr. Mason, "get a *good* one." And then, the well worn slogan, "The best is none too good for us." Furniture was ordered right from Wanamaker's in Philadelphia. Waiters were imported from the same seat of modest elegance. And the barber shop! None of your home talent for the mirrored barber shop. Gotlieb himself was imported and installed before the gold-lettered shaving mugs which stood (and stood till the hotel was burned in 1935) in their cubbyholes, flanking the mirrors. Gotlieb ruled the shop in a manner befitting his Teutonic name until he was succeeded by my good colored friend Avery. In the consulship of Avery, the shop was the open forum of free speech: political, economic, social, and futuristic. If only I could reach out into the ether waves and capture the Rabelaisian wit and the Socratic wisdom that went on the air while Avery administered Fitch shampoo, I could write a Tacoma anthology that would epitomize the sum and substance of an age when America felt as young as she was. Barber shops aren't what they used to be — what with manicures and women and such.

Hotel visitors swapped tales of magnificence.

"Got a potato peeler run by steam, by God!"

"Yep, an' they got an oven big enough to bake five hundred loaves of bread an' two hundred an' fifty pies!"

"Jeez! Have ye seen th' bar?"

Seattle and Portland had been watching, waiting, counting the days. Envy and curiosity lured the rivals to manager Tyler's grand opening. They strolled about the spacious lobby, practicing the feel of hotel habituées.

"Where's the water closet?" asked a Seattleite.

"Fourth spittoon to the left, sir," answered the ready bellhop.

The hotel, with its dignified, ample spaces, extended a welcome in the outstretched hand of the greeter behind the desk.

"Sorry, sir, but we're just plumb full up."

"No, the hall's all full up with cots right now. Sorry, sir."

" 'Fraid not, sir. Billiard tables all occupied. What? No place to sleep? *Well* now! That's just too bad. Have you tried the Rostwick?"

From the bar, which was finished first, to the yet-unfinished top story, the place was packed. The widespread lobby echoed to the sound of dancing feet and the voices of speculators in corner lots, predicting, predicting, predicting, Mason's Addition, Baker's Addition, Coulter's Addition, had but yesterday been put on the market. Brown's Addition would go on tomorrow, and, already, prospective investors were jockeying for a place in line. Buy quick; sell quick; put the proceeds into Jones's; sell again and shoot the works into Robinson's.

Trades were made between drinks and deeds were signed between dances. A bright new Eldorado had been discovered. Some magic of psychology would keep it glowing in the mists. The city was built upon a hill: it could not be hid.

CHAPTER VII

THE SWITCHBACK OVER Stampede Pass was a fearsome expedient. It was expensive to operate, and, what was more to the point, it was too slow for a community all geared up to high speed. While the first trains were puffing up under full steam and skidding down on screaming brakes, the engineers were making daring plans for the Stampede tunnel. The contract for the bore was given to Nelson Bennett, a two-fisted American, ready and eager to

> Shake the iron hand of fate
> And match with destiny for bears.

The very name of the pass suggested its forbidding character. A gang of trail-cutters, employed by the first engineer-explorers, turned tail, quit, and stampeded before the difficulties, leaving only one boy in the camp. He was not a quitter. Left alone, he chalked the name *Stampede Camp* on a bit of board, nailed it to a tree, and stuck to his job.

With the contract in his pocket, Mr. Bennett telegraphed the news, and it reached the ears of George Francis Train in New York. Citizen Train, as he loved to call himself, was alight with enthusiasm over the future of the new city. BORE BENNETT BORE! BORE BENNETT BORE! he telegraphed. It sounded like drum taps. It became a marching song echoed across the country. The applause stimulated the eccentric Train to further publicity for Tacoma — and for himself.

Citizen Train was a poet, one of the unintelligent poets of the day whose imagination leapt behind the confines of familiar phrases and who, in consequence, found a vogue among the intellectual elite. He took Tacoma for his theme song. The workings of his mind were as unrestricted as his verse. He conceived the grand idea of proving to the world that there was no spot on earth from which and to which the routes of world travel radiated so naturally as Tacoma.

54

Reporter Nellie Bly had just beaten the record of Jules Verne's Phineas Fogg around the world, making it in seventy-two days, six hours, eleven minutes, and fourteen seconds.

"Ah," said Train, "but she didn't start from Tacoma, the geographical center of the world. Put up the money and I'll do it from Tacoma *to* Tacoma, and I'll do it in sixty days." He scribbled a note on the back of a menu card in a New York restaurant: "Why not sell the Tacoma Theater for a thousand dollar lecture, and I'll start from Tacoma and land back in Tacoma in sixty days."

As editor Arthur Brisbane used to say, "What men can imagine, men can do." The dream in those days was transmuted into reality with no loss of time. The *Ledger* sponsored the scheme. Allen C. Mason pushed it by contributing his real estate salesman, Major Stamm, who acted as auctioneer for the theater ticket sale. Under the picturesque Major the house was sold out, boxes, seats, and standing room. An inadvertent nod toward the auctioneer cost General Sprague five hundred and twenty-five dollars, the price of the first box. Whiz bang! Citizen Train was financed to the tune of three thousand three hundred and ninety-five dollars.

"Train's train!" was announced in headlines by every crossroads town across the country, as it bore the hero to his starting point. This was publicity plus. The Northern Pacific was quick to see the advertising value and made the most of it. The Tacoma *Ledger* screamed the news in bigger and even better type. Crowds gathered before the *Ledger* office to get the latest bulletins of the receptions along the way. Merchants outdid each other in contributing going way gifts for the Great American Traveler: shirts and shoes; *multum in parvo* bags and money belts; the new and stylish long-legged balbriggan underwear; and, a marvel of ingenuity, a stylographic (fountain) pen.

Tacoma's very liquid sunshine greeted Train's train, as, with screeching brakes, its whistle valve wide open and its bell ringing, it came down the steep grade. The most opulent-looking carriage in town, drawn by four gray horses, carried the globe-circler to the theater, where he began his lecture by asking that the gas jet footlights be turned low. He allowed that he would furnish all the gas that was needed. So inflated was he that he had enough gas left for a second lecture for the overflow which filled Germania Hall.

The start was to be made from the *Ledger* office, and a huge brass plate commemorating the event was put up outside the building.

Early in the morning the carriage with four prancing horses was drawn up before the tablet. Train was on his mark at the starting place. The official timekeepers stood by, watches in hand. The start was announced by the booming of a gun on the bluff. Train leaped from the commemorative tablet into the carriage. The driver lashed the horses, and the timekeepers followed. Geysers of mud drenched the cheering onlookers as the cavalcade dashed down Pacific Avenue to the wharf, where the stern wheeler *Olympian*, shivering under her steam pressure, lay with her lines already cast off and her bow pointed toward the straits. Amid the booming of the old Russian cannon and the screeching of whistles, Train jumped from dock to deck, his newly-acquired outfit was heaved after him, and the timekeepers consulted their watches.

"Six minutes of the sixty days," announced Ike Anderson. "He'll make it sure."

The transpacific liner *Abyssinia* stuck her nose into the Royal Roads off Victoria, coming abreast of the *Olympian*. Train was hauled aboard, a few appropriate words accompanied the breaking of a bottle of wine over the bow, and the first leg of the race was on.

True to his instinct for the picturesque, Train cast the log of his argosy into the sea in tightly corked bottles; and by a freak of luck, the first bottle was carried by the flowing tide to the hand of an Indian who, sensing the importance of the thing, took it to a nearby cannery, whence it was carried to Tacoma. Cast off in mid-ocean, it carried the single word of ambition, PROGRESS.

The next word was a cryptic cable reading CONNECTED, but not until much later did Tacoma hear the fantastic story covered by that one word. At Yokohama, where Train was to connect with the North German Lloyd ship for Hong Kong, he learned that the *General Werder* had sailed two days before and was then docked at Kobe. It was Good Friday, and the German agent for the line was celebrating the holy day, German fashion, in bed. He was routed out and in the name of Tacoma was told to have the ship held until Train could reach Kobe by rail. Herr Leopold listened to Don Quixote and, convinced of the importance to the world of this journey, he ordered the ship held. Train spent the day getting his passport in order, involving, according to his modest claims, the intervention of the emperor himself. "Three days to sign a paper!" said Train. "It's time we reduced the limit to three minutes." He dashed off to

Tokyo, got the signature (so he said) of the All Highest (nobody asked what it looked like), and took the train for Kobe where he boarded the German vessel.

Train leapt around the world like a kangaroo. He leapt from steamer to sampan, from sampan to rickshaw, and from rickshaw to whatever of the picturesque he could find. The story of the flight on the magic carpet couldn't have seemed more like an Arabian Night's tale than the list of the names of the strange ports into and out of which he bounded. The name of Tacoma was carried to Hong Kong, Singapore, Colombo, and the Gulf of Aden; to Port Said and Brindisi. It reverberated in Rome and Paris and in London, where he told the wondering English of the City of Destiny. There he leapt again to the deck of the *Etruria* and, days later, he leapt from the *Etruria's* deck to New York's dock, where, so sure was he of the momentous import of his mission, he fully expected to find a special train with steam up waiting for him.

Alas! after having jousted against the windmills of the world, Don Quixote's lance failed to pierce the apathy (skullduggery, he called it) of his fellow American boosters. There was no special train. There was only a crowd of reporters who sensed good (and funny) copy. The depth of humiliation came when he found that on the last triumphant leg of his flight he had been routed over the Union Pacific to his hated rival, Portland, instead of over the Northern Pacific to his beloved terminus, Tacoma.

And he lost his pocketbook, too. And he didn't discover his loss till he tried to pay for a banquet to which he had invited all the newspapermen within reach of his voice.

Poor knight errant! I tell the story with a sympathetic understanding in my response to his world-conquering spirit. There is a good bit of the screwball in me, a remnant, perhaps, born in my early Tacoma days, and so it hurts me to think of this super screwball coming home to find "the last for which the first was made" all flattened out like a flounder. His fellow madmen had turned their attention to the formation of the "Pacific League of Professional Baseball Players." The scareheads on the *Ledger* just passed the globetrotter up, and he opened his paper to read:

CANNONADING CONTEST
SPOKANE SLUGGERS SLICK STICK SLINGING
TACOMA THOROUGHLY TROUNCED

The official timekeepers went into a huddle and announced that Train's time around the world was sixty-seven days, twelve hours, fifty-nine minutes, and fifty-five seconds. In vain he protested that his actual traveling time, while not asleep on waiting room benches was fifty-nine days and seven hours. But it was no good.

"Can it be," Citizen Train asked sadly, "that, after all, my life is in the past? I cannot understand it unless it be that I have accomplished all that there is for me to do. To think of the plans I had — all around the world! There seems to be nothing left for me but to return to silence."

His last days were spent feeding the sparrows in the park in New York and watching their wings, dreaming of his own.

CHAPTER VIII

EVERY DAY WAS New Year's day in Tacoma, but the old fashion of observing the first of January still prevailed, and the *Ledger* spread itself with jubilant editorials, the first day of 1891.

> The remarkable figures in today's issue powerfully indicate the future of Tacoma. Not in the spirit of vain panegyric has it been styled the City of Destiny. Its rise to Metropolitan greatness and worldwide fame within a few brief years has been one of the romances of the nineteenth century. . . . From amidst a sombre forest of firs, a city has arisen as by a stroke of an enchanter's wand. Like a new Venice, Tacoma looks forth over the glassy waters and prepares to handle the commerce of the world. For thousands of leagues, white sails glisten on the sea, bearing to this mart the fabrics of many lands, and to bear away in exchange the heat, coal, lumber and other bounteous products of this magnificent clime. . . . The new year will witness greater wonders in this regard than created amazement in the year that has just passed. Let ENERGY! AMBITION! and ENTERPRISE! continue to give lustre to the City of Destiny.

Abe Gross's store was no longer the only brick store in town, for, as the *Ledger* stated, among the "remarkable figures," there were "twenty-nine brick buildings all going up at the same time." But Abe didn't worry. He trimmed his windows for the New Year's Day, and the window dressing was a marvel of artistry. In one window there was a Romeo and Juliet scene, Juliet tricked out in some of those "fabrics of many lands" while in the other there appeared a sturdy blacksmith shop, all done in lace. The display stimulated the *Ledger* all over again.

The old Alpha Opera House, which had stood on Pacific Avenue for seven years (although we measured time by events, not by the discreet ticking of the clock), went the way of the tough and the picturesque. It had been opened with *Muldoon's Picnic,* followed by Modjeska in *Camille,* and, in turn, by Henry Ward Beecher on his favorite topic, "The Italy of America," when a drenching rain dropped its curtain over the Italian skies during his lecture. John L. Sullivan, the Boston strong boy, had followed with his rib-smashings, and with that chaste performance the glory of the old house faded. The day when we could be "nice" and tough at the same time was passing. A bank — looking, as all banks must, like a Greek temple — settled its respectable bulk on the site where the old house had stood.

Romeo and Juliet, looking from Abe's display window across the street of planks, saw the opening of the new Tacoma Theater, built for the migrant flux of forty thousand souls, big enough and grand enough for the wildest dreams of a census taker.

Fresh from the modest splendors of the Rutland Opera House, I read, with swelling heart:

BRILLIANT INAUGURAL   SEASON OF COMIC OPERA
CHORUS OF SIXTY   COMPLETE ORCHESTRA
J. C. DUFF'S COMIC OPERA COMPANY
FIRST PRODUCTION HERE OF THE LATEST
COMIC OPERA SUCCESS
PAOLA!
By the Composers of Ermine

The house was jam-packed with what Ike Striker called a "hot stuff" audience. The *Ledger* went to press late and spoke:

'TWAS A GALA NIGHT
TACOMA'S NEW THEATER OPENED WITH SPLENDOUR
COMPLETE IN DETAILS
FURNITURE AND FITTINGS CALL FOR ADMIRATION
THE SEASON'S SOCIAL EVENT
A GAY THRONG OF TACOMA'S YOUTH AND BEAUTY
BEAUTIFUL TOILETTES WORN
ALL PLEASED WITH THE FINEST PLAY HOUSE IN THE WEST

The curtain was tastefully adorned with what the scene painter called a "speaking likeness of the Temple of Diana." It served as a criterion of fine art for many years, as it unrolled itself again and again for a succession of the favorites of the day. Louise Baudet came and the old barnstormer, Frederick Warde. Levy, the cornetist who blew his cornet at the opening of the Brooklyn Bridge, came — and I can produce his double tonguing today, with a drop of saliva on the end of my tongue. And then — with a mountain of scenery, properties, and wardrobe trunks — The Emma Juch Grand Opera Company rolled into town for a season of nine nights and matinees. The season opened with *Faust*, Mme. Juch playing Marguerite. The next morning, after the first performance, Mme. Juch was taken for a ride over the plank roads for a sightseeing tour. So charmed was she that she fell for the wiles of the real estate man, took a thousand-dollar flyer in corner lots, and left Tacoma, nine days later with a thousand-dollar profit.

The classic art of Mme. Juch was followed by Nellie McHenry — rowdy, indecorous, and wholly delightful, in *Skip by the Light of the Moon*. My taste is low; it has always been low. I loved seeing her swish her skirts about, show her garters, and shout "Rubber!" at the front-row boys. And I knew Nellie. During my glee club days at Yale, we sang one unforgettable concert in St. Louis on New Year's Eve. At the Old Hotel Southern, after the concert, we fell in with Nellie and her troupe together with Sol Smith Russell and his company. These glamorous professionals suggested that we Yale boys join up with our brother troupers and see the New Year in with them. Nellie was at her unconventional best. Under her stimulus I drank much champagne. I remember that, though I do not remember finding my room afterward. When Nellie came to Tacoma, I did a bit of modest boasting of what I called my friendship with the lady. I gained a brief reputation as a gay dog among those whose reputation was already made, but it didn't help me any with the pure posh on Nob Hill.

At the rear of the theater, appropriately named, ran Opera Alley where Blanche, Julie, and French Fifine did a thriving business — their names painted on their doors in gaudy letters, the ladies soliciting custom in the open windows. The wide doors of the theater flanked the entrance to Opera Alley. You could avert your eyes, bayward, as you went in, or you could risk one eye on the street of sin. The choice was an embarrassing one. Most of us did both.

Richard Mansfield came with his repertory company to make us feel that we were not more than one hop behind New York. He played Beau Brummell and Dr. Jekyll and Mr. Hyde. Then he met McLaren Post, and his heart went the way of all young hearts at that susceptible time. While I dreamed of the lovely McLaren, Richard *acted*. I hadn't a Chinaman's chance. Richard had more than dreams and roses to give.

"I do so wish," said McLaren, "that I could see you in *Prince Carl*."

"Dear lady," said Richard, "you shall. I shall give you a theater party and you shall invite the house."

For *Social Register* we had only the *Polk Directory* — and even that was in its first edition. McLaren rushed at it; and thumbed it for her guests. I got an invitation to come in white tie and tails, and to bring all the white tie and tailed friends I could muster. The invitation list was compiled by geometric progression. If you have ten friends with white tie and tails and each friend has ten, you have the makings of a real theater party. The boxes were filled with the socially elect, so I never got near one but I did get a seat down in front where I worshipped McLaren as she swept into her box, radiant in white, half hidden in Richard's roses. Between the acts, I met Ike Striker, dressed in what he called "a full evening dress suit," which he had hired from a waiter.

The painted Temple of Diana eventually yielded to modern curtains. Buskin and trappings on the boards, white tie, and the toilette in the orchestra — all gave way to the Hollywood screen across the proscenium and sports clothes in the audience. Tacoma then could go six nights a week to see the flicker of Hollywood stars — and forget them — for the price of one gorgeous night when we could see beauty in the flesh, and remember. I suppose it's all right — oh, yes, I suppose so. One must get used to the thought that "there is nothing nature loves so well as to change existing forms and to make new ones like them."

But I could do once more with a taste of the bubbling well of enthusiasm, sweet and heady, on tap for the young men and women of a new town.

CHAPTER IX

TOMORROW, STILL ANOTHER platted addition would be put on the market, with streets all nicely graded with a plow, sidewalks built with planks on stilts, and a scattering of half-built houses around which carpenters made a great to-do with hammer and saw. This was a come-on device of the operator.

"That? Oh, that house is being rushed for Mr. Whoozis, He got in early, the lucky cuss. An' see that residence over there, the round one with the round tower and the finials? That belongs to Mr. What's-his-name. Goin' to have him a Spanish "patois" in it. Quite a pretentious little home, ain't it?"

Long before the advertised hour, a far reaching line, with its head in the office door, waited for an early selection of a choice lot. By being on the spot bright and early, you could buy an option on a corner lot, and you could sell your option at a fat profit. You could even sell your place in line for fifty dollars and scoot around to the rear of the procession, sure that still another slug-abed would appear and buy your place again.

We went, Father and I, to have a look. I champed the bit with eagerness to buy a lot next to the "pretentious little home," but the Vermont halter and the Vermont purse were still held by Father. We inspected the half-built house of Mr. What's-his-name, he of the Spanish patois, and while I admired the hand-sawed ornaments and the spindles, Father had a look at the wooden foundations.

"Knowledge and timber shouldn't be much used till they are seasoned," Father quoted, and as he turned toward the roadway, "Wisdom crieth *without*: she uttereth her voice in the street."

I did so want to join these progressive fellows and make some easy money; my secretary's salary of a hundred a month was so humdrum. We were the terminus (by this time I was saying "we"), and not only of the Northern Pacific — that was old stuff. The Union Pacific was spending millions grading its right of way to Tacoma from Portland. Surely Sam Wilkenson was justified in his prediction to Nay Cooke. The EMPIRE OF THE PACIFIC was already established on Puget Sound, and God himself had said, "Let there be Tacoma." And the Canadian Pacific was casting a covetous eye our way too. Didn't we see it in print?

"There is no possible reason to doubt," said the *Ledger*, "that, at no distant date, the Canadian Pacific will be running from Quebec direct to Tacoma. Late developments have shown that the recent visit of President Vahorne of the *Canadian Pacific Railroad Company*, to Tacoma, was not *wholly* for *pleasure*." (The italics are *not* mine.) When the president of the Canadian Pacific came to visit our town and looked mysterious, it was obvious that soon dirt would begin to fly. And soon after that, the proud ships of the Empress Line would be seeking dock facilities on Commencement Bay. We were the natural terminus of all the railroads of North America and of the shipping lanes of the seven seas.

Jim Hill of the Great Northern had come, too. The Chamber of Commerce had stretched itself on the grandest dinner that the imagination of the Tacoma Hotel could compass. We called Jim Hill EMPIRE BUILDER! in an electric sign ten feet high and forty feet long. The chaste magnificence of the Lucullan whoopee had moved Jim to tears. But if the tables were loaded, Jim wasn't. We had expected that Hill would beg admission to the city on a right of way, bought at an exorbitant price; but the Empire Builder was cagey. In his speech, he "hoped the city would make the most of its *agricultural possibilities!*"

"Agriculture, hell!" snorted we, who had paid for the champagne. "Does Jim Hill think we are a bunch of farmers? Ain't we got the longest wheat warehouses in the world? Ain't we got the Northern Pacific back of us? An' the Tacoma Land Company? Ain't we got all the natural facilities for manufacturing in the world? We should worry."

But Seattle whooped with joy: "Watch Tacoma grow — spuds on Pacific Avenue!"

"Ain't we the 'open see-saw' to the Pacific?" asked Ike Striker, knocking together his row of "bungaloos" on K Street.

"Pacific Ocean's jest our back yard."

Bill Owen, fresh from the coast of Maine, looked up from his job of nailing cresting to the ridge pole, a Yankee twist to his mouth and a Yankee twinkle in his eye. He squinted across the burned slashing

*"The groves,
which yesterday were
God's first temples,
are being shaped into
uncouth, false-fronted
temples of whiskey
and provender . . ."*

The land was rich in sweeping stands of timber and Tacomans seized upon them as bounty provided by a foresightful Providence. The great trees were felled and hauled to the mills of Puget Sound, where they were transformed by a "maelstrom of whirring machinery" into doors, sashes, shingles, brackets, cresting, spindles, porch columns, and finished lumber for the building of a city and the commerce of the world.

"Move grandly on, thou car of fate,
Deep freighted with a rich estate.
Tacoma's dealers need not fear;
The land is here—it is all here!"

Above: Logging operations near Shelton in the 1890's.

Below: Hansen & Co.'s Tacoma Mill, a "voracious Gargantua, swallowing the growth of centuries at a gulp and spewing out the digested product."

The Wallace Wood camp, near Shelton.

The product and crew of a shingle mill.

"We were no heroes of a western movie. We were just a crew of young men, drawn together in the common purpose to 'grow up with the country . . .'"

to the waters of the bay. "Yuss — I see 'tis," he said. He shifted his quid and turned his back to put on another length of cresting.

"Bill," said Ike, "ain't you State o' Maine fellers got any imagination? Ain't you got any vision? Lookit here." He unfolded a frayed bit of newspaper clipping.

> The happy holder of one of these corner lots can see on his right majestic Mount Tacoma, lifting its snow capped peak fourteen thousand, four hundred and forty-four feet into the clouds. On his left he can glimpse the serrated peaks of the Olympic Range, while the commerce of the world passes and repasses in endless pageant at his feet.

Bill whanged another nail into the cresting and looked bayward. "By gum! There goes the commerce o' th' world," he said, as the old stern-wheeler *State of Washington* churned her way around Brown's Point.

"*Phra Nang's* comin' tomorrow," said Ike. "Passed Cape Flattery, paper says. She's loaded with all the spices o' th' Orient — 'n silk 'n tea 'n things. Goin' to load wheat fer the starvin' Chinks. Ever see anything like *that* in Maine? Dum Yankee!"

The *Phra Nang*, advance guard of the commerce of the world, drifted in the next morning to the tooting of every whistle in town. Charles E. Marvin, chairman of the reception committee, boarded her from a naphtha launch with a brass band that rent the air as lines were thrown to the longest wheat warehouse in the world. The astonished Yorkshire captain came ashore. He had tied up at the major ports of the world's oceans without seeing anything like this. He was hoisted to the deck of a flatcar, where he listened to Marvin's eulogy of Tacoma.

The red-rusted British tramp had an eye painted, Chinese fashion, on her bows. "With that eye to guide her," said Marvin, "that gallant ship has smelled her way from far Cathay to her natural home port." The mixed metaphor went unheeded. Sight and smell were all the same to the crowd of Tacomans who whooped their welcome. And no one reflected that the natural home port of the sea wanderer was wherever tea and silks, jute and nitrates, Japanese fans and imitation pearls could be found and exchanged for coal, wool, bicycles, and rubber boots, quite as well as for wheat and lumber. The Captain, embarrassed beyond words, responded. He said, "Thankee—thankee."

"The longest wheat warehouse in the world" stood at the water's edge below the bluff for all to see from the terrace of the Tacoma Hotel. And there, shortly, true to Ike Striker's prediction, floated a visible portion of the "commerce of the world." A flotilla of sailing ships lay alongside the dock, a mountain of wheat disappearing into their holds from trucks pushed by sweating stevedores. The big windjammer *A. G. Ropes*, carrying, the *Ledger* said, eight thousand yards of canvas, made port from Yokohama in only thirty days to discharge "three thousand seven hundred and seventy-five tons of tea." Young Vermont, whose notion of ships was limited to a rowboat on Otter Creek, was charmed by such an inordinate amount of canvas and tea, but I was more thrilled by the aroma of cordage and tar and all the other smells of a ship. There were salt-water sailors too, and a first mate bawling orders, and the grunt and whine of the loading tackle.

Headlines, and a new editorial rhapsody, appeared next morning in the *Ledger*:

> Portland's star as an exporting place has been declining as ours has passed to the ascendant, and the late storms have given her a reputation in this respect, a bad blow. While it is not generous or commendable to exult over the misfortunes of a rival, it is entirely praiseworthy to recognize the advantages of our position and make the most of it. The storms which have so seriously damaged the reputation of the Columbia have tremendously benefited ours as ships have come and gone without difficulty, and those in our harbor have enjoyed complete security.

"The commerce of the world, passing and re-passing in endless pageant at our feet!" We include in our count the fleet of Siwash canoes, loaded to the gunwales with mixed families of braves, klootchmans, and papooses. Singing to the rhythmic beat of their paddles, from the outer world of the reservation they came for the hop-picking. With a mighty splash, they grounded the big dugout canoes on the mud flats near the warehouse and within sound of the *hiu-chick-chick* of the railroad. They threw out blankets, bark, baskets, blackjack, and babies in one riot of color and strong smells, and set up their cozy housekeeping in the ooze of the tide flats.

The squaws squatted about their tiny fires and went on with their weaving of bark mats and baskets without missing a beat, while the braves went to town in search of whisky and the rubber boots that were the badge of the Indian on a night out in town. The babies sprawled on the beach where they had landed on being thrown out.

The Indian woman at home in her camp is quite unlike the solemn squaw one sees squatting on the curb, selling her baskets. Among her own, she is as gay and talkative over her weaving as are her white sisters at the sewing circle on Nob Hill. And she doesn't let her social proclivities interfere with her duty to the babies, either. Her conception of child psychology is embodied in the one simple rule: "Have 'em, love 'em, and leave 'em be." And with this apparent calm neglect, she exercises a patient control that is the despair of the new generation of white mothers.

Ike Striker, contractor and observer, thought that white wives might learn something else from the Siwash women, for when the brave returned from his shopping expedition with the new rubber boots on his feet and the whisky filling his skin, the fond klootchman sang cuddlesome little notes of joy and pride as she laid him out on the wet sand and called the other squaws to look.

Affecting the easy familiarity of the old-timer, I strolled among the Indians and stopped where a squaw was picking a half-raw smelt from a rusty saucepan.

"Skookum?" I asked, using the language of the country — the only word of Chinook I had learned. It didn't go over big at all.

"Klatawa! Klatawa!" said the lady — and I got out, which I rightly guessed was what she meant; and it was obvious that she *meant* what she meant. You may talk down to a humble native of rural France, in your high school French, and get a veneer of politeness in response; but don't affect the friendly *grand seigneur* with the Indian, or you're in for a good snubbing.

CHAPTER X

THE INSTINCT FOR A DECENT and orderly life was deeply rooted in the community and very early sent up green shoots from the compost heap of heterogeneous material. In the early years, the town was pretty much built about the saloon and the brothel, and shootings were common bits of daily news. I came too late for all that. I saw only one shooting, and it was not a pretty sight: a poor derelict running from the door of a saloon and crumpling up on the sidewalk with three slugs in him.

On the aesthetic side, the Territorial Legislature had long before passed a law entitled "An Act to Prevent the Owners of Hogs from Running at Large." Without discriminating between the hogs and their owners, public opinion found expression in an editorial:

> Mr. Graham will do the public a great favor and himself credit by hereafter keeping those bothersome pigs, which he is rearing at the expense and annoyance of the public, in a proper enclosure. It is bad enough to keep the animals within hearing and smelling distance, but when they are eternally sticking their noses into every open door in the vicinity, and chasing after every man, woman, or child who carries a basket or bucket near their habitation, and, at the same time squealing in deafening chorus for something to eat, it is high time the public should ask him to abate his nuisance.

The pigs having been disposed of, the first Literary Society was formed. While the tough boys in the lower town were still drinking, gambling, and brawling over dissolute women, elsewhere thoughts soared upward. High up on a bluff where the more rarefied air better suited the Attic philosophy, the élite launched the society in the topmost story of the only schoolhouse in town. The place was reached from the bay by what was known for many years as the "202 steps," and it was a weary climb. Once there, the windblown founders elected all the officers to be found in the book of parliamentary procedure, with titles for all. There was a president, a vice president, a secretary, a treasurer, an editor, a sergeant at arms, and a critic, whose all-encompassing job was strenuous. Uplift was on the march, and it found expression in the little group which wrestled culture with a half Nelson, and threw it.

Though the women had sponsored the movement, no woman held office. Only a rumor of the feminist movement had been heard across the Cascades, and that was, as Ike Striker said, "all blah!" When the men of the town heard of the battle of the "pantaloonatics" in the East, the frequenters of Pacific Avenue chanted:

> Hush little baby, don't get in a fury,
> 'Cause Mama's gone to sit on a jury.

Tennyson had been brought to Tacoma from the East, and there was a lot in Tennyson for a new town to quote. Mrs. Saltonstall-Sales, whose hyphenated name was spoken with reverence, read a paper beginning with a quotation that seemed to have been written especially for Tacoma:

> Broad-based upon her peoples' will
> And compassed by the inviolate sea.

Mr. Mason countered with a modest reference to his castle in Mason's Addition:

> I built my soul a lovely pleasure house
> Wherein, at ease, for aye to dwell.

The murmurous whisperings of the Browning Clubs of Boston were wafted across the country on the east wind. "In the morning of the world. . . . God's in His heaven: All's right with the world." And best of all, again introduced by Mrs. Saltonstall-Sales, was something about — what was it? Growing old with me? Yes. And, "The best is yet to be."

The meetings of the Literary Society were almost too highbrow for the men. As the meeting adjourned and they counted the "202 steps" to the lower levels, where the air was less rarefied, they drew deep breaths and voted that James Whitcomb Riley and Joaquin Miller, who had dawned on the horizon, came nearer the intellectual needs of the Pacific. Joaquin Miller's poems of the Sierra fairly exuded red blood, and Riley's homemade verse struck a nostalgic note in the hearts of the Hoosier element. The menfolk took it for granted that God was in his heaven, overlooking the best of all possible worlds. They didn't need to rhapsodize about it. Eugene Field, too, was writing the kind of verse which touched their daily lives. Down in Monty's saloon his unpublished "When Willie Wets His Bed" was passed about, and the stiff necks relaxed in good guffaws.

Up in the schoolhouse a telephone had been installed, and it was a marvel of efficiency. An arrangement was made with the operator in Olympia to hook up his instrument with the telegraph wires, just to see if the human voice could be carried that far. And it worked! A clarinet player in Olympia puckered his lips and played "Why Did They Dig Ma's Grave So Deep," and Tacoma gracefully responded with "There's Music in the Air."

This was to be no board-and-batten shack town, lacking the amenities of modern life, its men dragged down by the incessant, colorless fight for existence, its women leading drab and dreary lives, grey with dust and monotony. It was going to go in for every modern gadget as fast as it could be invented.

Hattie Wickwire, first lady of the underworld, had ceased to ride at the head of her regular Saturday afternoon parade advertising the attractions of her establishment, who followed her in carriages down Pacific Avenue and up C Street to where she operated in Opera Alley. The forces of decency had relegated Hattie to her own business quarters.

Harry Morgan's house of gambling and what-not was still going strong. A meeting was called to consider this wicked but fascinating enterprise. There was much oratory. An earnest citizen, a natural and willing symposiarch, raised his voice for the social and moral benefit of the city, and he didn't omit the promise of financial betterment that would follow the uplift of morals. He thought that Harry Morgan, with his "box rustlers" and other facilities for sin, should be condemned as a public nuisance, even if it did mean the loss of the best brass band in the West. "A disgrace to the fair name of our city," he called it. His audience listened, impressed but reluctant. Virtue was all right in its way but Ike Striker thought "Mebbe it's kind o' outlived its usefulness." No one quite dared to take issue with the earnest citizen on the question of civic virtue. There was an outward show of pious indignation over the vice which was played up by the band, but an inward satisfaction with the flow of foreign money over the tables and into the stockings of the box rustlers. The earnest citizen's clarion call to rectitude was interrupted by a practical bombshell, thrown right into the procession of the righteous. Another citizen, of tempered righteousness, jumped to his feet.

"I rise to suggest," he said, "that the question be laid on the table."

"Aye," voted the meeting in a somewhat subdued voice.

"No," roared the earnest citizen.

"The ayes have it," announced the chairman.

The meeting adjourned. Lofty purpose had been served and a profitable industry had been saved.

"Anyway," said Ike Striker, "we've a city now, an' such things always go with a city. It's turrible, o' course, but I guess we just can't help it."

Our Vermont hearts swelling with holy indignation, our Vermont minds filled with unholy curiosity about the inside works of a western vice joint, brother Will and I left the meeting and solemnly pondered the matter. And as we pondered, we drifted, as though drawn by a magnet, toward Morgan's Palace of Pleasure. Doctor Parkhurst, president of the Society for the Suppression of Crime, was waging war against sin in New York, and he was attacking sin on the inside, where the sin was. Carrie Nation was attacking Demon Rum in the Middle West, and she was attacking rum on the inside, where rum was. Shouldn't we join the crusade and attack the inside lines of sin on the West Coast? Will thought we ought to know just how bad this thing was before we attacked. I thought so too.

Will said, "We shouldn't go into this thing blindly; we ought to see with our own eyes." I was all for that. Will said, "You can't go around hollering about vice till you know how much vice there is — and what kind."

I said, "Sure, it's our duty."

Up on the balcony, the Harry Morgan band was blowing "The Stars and Stripes Forever," as we wedged our way into the crowd about the doorway. Assuming the easy swagger of the West, we went in.

In the front room stood "the longest bar north of San Francisco," with its brass rail at the foot and mangy-looking towels hanging down at intervals along the front. Beer slopped over the top, making an easy runway, along which the barkeep slid the schooners with amazing accuracy, to stop just in front of the thirsty lumberjack. There was a happy-go-lucky crowd, all pleasantly paying the wages of sin in the come-easy, go-easy way of loggers.

At the rear, discreetly hidden by a partition, you could lose your wad in a bewildering variety of games. It was hard to choose, for neither Will nor I had ever played "for keeps" anything more complicated than marbles. We studied the operation of the roulette table, and then Will, with the air of a hardened old rounder, tossed a dollar on the red — and won.

A nice-looking man stood behind the shallow, green-lined box covered with a glass top. On the green lining were stacks of hard money: silver dollars, five-dollar gold pieces, and a scattering of twenty-dollar coins, each stack topped by a number. The dealer, a charming fellow with a black mustache and a fancy waistcoat, was kindness itself. He explained that, for a dollar, I could throw a box full of dice, and if I threw a number corresponding to a number in the box, the pile of gold under it would be mine.

"It's simple," he said and added, in a discouraged way, that his luck wasn't very good just then. I hesitated. A man in a derby hat and a diamond stickpin stepped in and threw the dice. With amazing speed, the dealer counted the spots and passed over ten dollars.

"That's the way it's mostly goin' today," the dealer said. "Lady Luck's deserted me. Want to try a throw before I get cleaned out?" I passed out my silver dollar, shook the dice, and threw. Again the dealer exhibited his skill in the speedy addition of spots and swept the dice off the board before I could begin to add. I had hardly begun my stuttering protest when Jumbo Cantwell, a very big man, began to push me about — very gently, to be sure, but firmly.

"Better get th' hell out o' here," he said.

Descensus in Averno facile est — the descent into hell is very easy. Will and I went down a few steps to the rear and sidled into the Theater Comique, which was the most profitable part of Harry Morgan's business. A hearty blonde, ungirdled, dressed to reveal much and suggest more, greeted us most hospitably.

"Looky, who's here," she crowed. "College boys! Come and 'ave a drink." She hustled us into a box which was snugly draped with curtains. "What's yours, baby?"

"Beer," said Will.

"Same for me," said I.

The big girl brought three bottles and three cloudy mugs. "Three dollars, dears," she said. She slipped the money into her stocking and looked us over. As Will, with his beard, looked more like easy money than I did, she draped herself over his lap. Will looked helpless and, with his idle hands, acted helpless.

"What's the matter, baby?" asked the hustler. "Ain't this what you come for?"

Will untangled himself. "Guess we don't want any beer after all," he said. "Come on, Tom. We've got to be going."

We escaped through the gambling room and past the long bar, followed by a shout of "short sport" from our hostess.

In spite of our careful investigation, Will and I had no part in the ousting of Harry Morgan. In fact, there wasn't any ousting. The rowdy frontier town was learning good taste and good manners without violent action. Harry Morgan didn't need proscription by the city fathers to know when he had had enough. There were already laws aplenty, far too many, in fact. There was a law prohibiting the sale, purchase, or smoking of cigarettes. We bought Bull Durham and rolled our own and smoked on the quiet. There was a law against treating to drinks. "Gimme a whisky. What's yours?" "I'll take a cigar, thank you." And then, cigar in hand, "I've changed my mind. Barkeep, want to swap a drink for a cigar?" "Any law against swappin'?" In the words of Mr. Bumble, "If the law supposes that, the law is a ass, a idiot." The mass of laws, so gaily and prolifically passed, never made Tacoma over into the delightful city it became. Like other joints that flourished so openly in the early days, Harry Morgan just folded up and disappeared before the invisible attacks which are always at work in our yet young America. The lusty community, kicking up its heels in sheer joy of its adolescent freedom, had blown some of its corks under pressure of its rapid fermentation.

With the passing of the more rip-roaring aspects of a young city, pulling itself out of the mire by its own bootstraps, there was still much to engage the attention of forward-looking youth, and we worked overtime at looking forward. Rubber tires, for instance, were revolutionizing our life. The progressive undertaker had equipped his hearse with solid rubber tires; and Sam Perkins, not to be out-done by a hearse, appeared in a rubber-tired carriage, which repre-sented the very spirit of quiet dignity. It made no noise at all as it rolled over the loose planks and squashed mud up between the cracks. We all admired it. Little Bobby Osgood flattened his nose against the window and announced its passing: "There goes Mr. Perkins' rubber-tired funeral!"

The old high-wheeled bicycle with its solid rubber tires had given way to the high-geared safety, rolling on rubber tires inflated with air, endangering life and property. The Tacoma Wheelman's Club, dressed in knee pants, was scorching about on the plank sidewalks. And now the women, mostly in bloomers — though the more brazen wore knee pants just like the men — claimed their right, too, to speed and distance. They organized the Ladies' Bicycle Club and went careering about. Boys and girls took to riding tandem, the girl up in front, the boy behind, his vision obscured by the girl's huge sleeves. There wasn't room for a chaperone. "How can you know where they go, or what they do when they get there?" was asked. "Answer me that!"

There was no limit to the marvels of the new age. Catalogues ad-vertised all sorts of new gadgets "for the most fastidious cyclist." You could get underslung handlebars with cork grips for the riders of the "century," a hundred miles, believe it or not, in a day. There were kerosene headlights, imperious sounding bells, clips for your trousers, and *multum in parvo* bags, with straps to go on your han-dlebars, to hold your nightgown and toothbrush for overnight runs to Olympia. The last word in refinement was the split saddle for ladies. The traffic problem was becoming hopeless.

The prairie to the south opened up a vast expanse of gravelly acreage where one could pedal at will, skirting the lovely lakes; but the bottleneck to the prairie, a steep coast down and a long push up, came at Delin's Gulch. The engineers got out their T squares and produced a plan for a bicycle bridge, and no bridge was ever planned with more zest. When it was completed, we touted it in the press as the "longest, highest, and *only* bicycle bridge in the world."

CHAPTER XI

"Two can live more cheaply than one." I don't know, today, whether the fellow who coined that aphorism deserved a roof, clothes, and a full stomach, or a park bench, rags, and the pangs of hunger. But as a swain in Tacoma, I swallowed the saying whole.

Charlotte and I had settled on six months as the period within which I would prove I could earn bed and board. As the time of our probation dragged along, I consulted my calendar with much more care than I gave to my bank balance, and put my faith in the Northern Pacific.

My letters to Charlotte were full of joyous pictures of Life in the West. "Soon," I wrote, "I will be filling your hands with these wonderful cherries."

Charlotte replied, "The cherries can wait. Can you?"

Somehow, the six months passed. I borrowed from my easygoing bank the price of one round-trip ticket to and from Rutland and enough to pay for a one-way ticket for a brand-new wife from Rutland back to Tacoma. This time, loyally, I chose for the eastern trip the Northern Pacific route through Nelson Bennett's Stampede Tunnel. For the wedding journey westward I chose the Union Pacific. I wanted to see the rising cities of the open lands on every transcontinental line that spanned the country.

Changing at Albany and again at Troy, I rolled into Rutland on the Central Vermont, and, as the Scotchman said upon arriving in Paris, "Bang went sixpence." I was met by ushers, hopefully waiting for Ascot ties and pins. And there were wedding presents: champagne glasses for a beer pocketbook; a huge silver loving cup — and lemonade to put into it; a silver mounted crop — and no horse to ride. It was a dazzling collection for a country boy who had been living on hopes, fresh air, and scenery. I counted my cash and then, in my perturbation, cut a gash in my chin while shaving.

Father sensed the impending ruin. "Have you enough money for all this?" he asked.

I didn't tell him of the loan I had negotiated. I held up my head and lied, "Yes, sir, thank you." But I hurried to the ticket office to buy Charlotte's one-way ticket to Tacoma while I had the price. The ticket agent studied maps and the mysterious books that ticket agents read.

"Tacoma? That ain't on our line, but you come back. We'll rastle 'er."

The rector of Trinity Church wanted everything done up all ship-shape. He wanted to bless the ring. He did. He put it on his little plate, and, in his sacramental fervor, he dropped it, and it went tinkling over the stone chancel floor. Brother Ned, my best man, stepped on it, then recovered it, and it found its blessed way to Charlotte's finger. We were pronounced man and wife to the accompaniment of a clap of thunder and a torrent of November rain. Ned held the umbrella as we hustled to the barouche. It was a tired bride that threw the bride's bouquet, a tired pair of innocents that boarded the train.

After a little while of dalliance in New England security, we set forth for Albany, for Troy, and for "Chicago and points west." At Omaha, the conductor looked at our tickets and then gave an appraising glance at Charlotte's palpably new going-away dress and her new initialed suitcase. He sat down on the Pullman seat with the air of an old uncle. "It's just too bad," he said, "but you, young man, are routed to Denver by the Rock Island, and your new wife has got to go by the U.P. Who routed you on your weddin' trip?"

"The ticket agent at Rutland, Vermont," I said.

"Guess he never heard of no place west o' Albany before," said he. "Got any money left? It'll cost you just forty-three dollars and seventy-five cents to go by the same route — one ticket and one berth, 'nless you want to go separate for one night." He looked troubled at the thought. "Me, I'd pay the price if I was you."

I paid the price. Meals and tips were very meager for the rest of the journey.

The bare and desolate Rocky Mountains had no fascination for a girl whose soul was knit unto Vermont's cozy Green Mountains. As peak after peak raised its barrier between her and her beloved Otter Creek Valley, she sighed, "Three thousand miles and three thousand dollars from Vermont." And as we rocked about the curves on the downgrade, symptoms of what I called car sickness appeared. A motherly old fellow passenger looked at Charlotte with that interested sympathy women always display under like circumstances.

"Feeling' kind o' squeamish in the mornin's?" she asked. "Never mind it, dearie; 'twon't last long, an' you'll be so happy when it comes."

"What did that meddling old woman say?" I asked.

"She said it," said Charlotte with a wan smile. "You — you *family* man!" She almost managed a laugh. "Do I make a good pioneer woman? Pity it couldn't be born on the plains — or at least in the baggage car."

"Hold everything," I said. "Look! We're going through the Royal Gorge! *Look!*"

We lurched around a curve between towering cliffs. Popeyed, I turned from the window, but Charlotte was on her staggering way to the end of the car. She never saw the Royal Gorge, but she got a vivid impression of it. She rechristened it, "The Royal Dis-Gorge."

There was another change at Salt Lake City and a night at the old Knutsford Hotel, very grand in its day; another racketing train on the Oregon Short Line; a last night at the comforting Hotel Portland; then the train ferry across the Columbia at Kalama, and we were in the state of our adoption. The mist didn't rise as a mist should; it came down, a remorseless drip, drip, drip, making muddy little rivulets on the grimy windows. Outside, black mud and black stumps combined in a scene dreary enough to make the hardiest pioneer wish he hadn't started.

No brass band met us as we pulled into the ramshackle station in Tacoma. I spent my last silver on a carriage that rattled us up to the Hotel Rochester, a kind of glorified boardinghouse, which was advertised to suit the modest purse and "the most fastidious tastes." It was eight o'clock and we were hungry. The dining room was hermetically sealed. A reluctant hostess prepared, with her own fair hands, two ham sandwiches and a bottle of milk.

"'O Captain! My Captain! Our fearful trip is done,'" quoted Charlotte.

CHAPTER XII

THE INTERREGNUM OF PRESIDENT HARRISON, between the two terms of Mr. Cleveland, ushered in the era of suavity in big business. Mr. Harrison was the very symbol of moral rectitude, and we were quite satisfied with the way things were going in the White House. Intent upon our own business, we failed to see the blackjack concealed in the silk sock.

The President made a tour of the West and stopped in Tacoma. We persuaded ourselves that he had arranged the long trip expressly to see us; we were convinced that his visit portended grand things for Tacoma, and so, with a lively sense of benefits to come, we prepared to express our loyal gratitude in advance. Flags and bunting came out of storage, and triumphal arches were knocked together to span the streets. Prancing horses were hitched to the most stylish carriages in town, and the President, followed by a cavalcade of lesser lights, was driven through the less unpresentable streets that he might see and admire Great Babylon which we had builded. We scanned the heavens for signs of rain, but we needn't have looked. The "Scotch mist" dropped a blanket over the whole show.

The First Lady, dry except for the bottom of her petticoats, was entertained in the foyer of the Tacoma Theater, which had been transformed into a sort of drawing room, with flowers and treasures borrowed from the homes of the élite. The ladies presented Mrs. Harrison with an original oil painting of Mount Tacoma, properly labeled.

"And please," said the ladies, "if you *must* go to Seattle, won't you call it by its right name and not Mount Rainier?"

The children were given a holiday from school. They lined up along the streets to be reviewed by the President, while anxious teachers rode herd on them.

"What are those children doing out here in the rain?" asked President Harrison. "Tell them to go home and be dried."

With water running down our coat collars, we cheered ourselves hoarse, but the President promised us no new railroads, no river and harbor improvements — nothing. A wag went home and wrote for the next morning's edition of the *Ledger*:

> Tacoma's rain was falling fast
> As up Pacific Avenue I passed
> A hatband underneath, a man
> Who muttered, as he only can,
> Drive faster!

In our enthusiasm over the impeccable moral atmosphere of the White House, we failed to see that things were going a bit haywire in the East. If some overextended business went to the wall in New York, it seemed to me merely the elimination of extra weight, which would leave the foundation of the business world all the better able to sustain the whole structure. I read, "The spectre of monopoly is showing its ugly head." So what? We, of Puget Sound, enjoying the vast gifts of land and timber, didn't recognize it as a monopoly; any one could "come and get it." But those fellows in steel and oil — well, that was different. Halfheartedly, I joined the chorus of voices from the farm states and shouted, "Down with the trusts!"

The clamor of the farm states grew, and the Sherman Anti-Trust Act was passed. It was designed to curb big business, curb the consumer, and lower the cost of living. Big business reeled into its corner, caught its breath, and staggered back into the ring with a new wallop: the McKinley Bill. I didn't then understand the economics of the McKinley Bill of prohibitive tariffs, and I don't now. It was said that the purpose of prohibitive tariffs was to shut off the importation of cheap goods (which we needed), and so reduce the revenue and so relieve the United States Treasury of its burden of surplus. I thought then that it was a strange relief from a strange sort of burden, and in later years, it seemed stranger still. But there that surplus was, a baffling and baleful thing.

Ike Striker, as usual, had his remedy, and he thought it was pretty good. "Why not take that surplus," asked Ike, "and pay that man McKinley his bill?"

By some strange alchemy, the McKinley Bill was to transform poverty into plenty. It would protect America's full dinner pail against the products of cheap foreign labor. Big business, now not too downcast over the Sherman Anti-Trust Act, while shutting the door to the products of the cheap foreign labor, opened it wide to cheap foreign laborers. By this action they would reduce wages again and so put the decencies of life within the reach of everybody but the fellows who produced them.

The decencies of life included pants, and the price of pants fell to three dollars. I can't today, repeat any of Shelley's "To a Skylark," but even after all these years, I can't get the three-dollar-pants jingle out of my head:

> When the pant hunter, pantless, is hunting for pants,
> And pants for the best pants the pant market grants,
> He panteth, unpanted, until he implants
> Himself in a pair of Plymouth Rock pants.

The Washington merry-go-round was whirling at a pace that would have made Drew Pearson dizzy.

To make confusion worse confounded, the Silver Purchase Act was passed. This measure, by some magic which again I didn't understand, would quiet the cries of the distressed farmer, while building up the fortunes of the silver states. What it did do was to hand out the gold of the Treasury to the smart one in the East, who promptly exchanged their silver certificates worth about sixty cents for Treasury notes worth a dollar. Gresham's Law promptly worked, as it always will. The bad money drove the good gold out of the Treasury in a steady stream. I had learned that much, at least, from Billy Sumner at Yale.

Ambrose Bierce, the mysterious philosopher who shortly disappeared from our ken, gave form to the enthusiastic muddle of our social philosophy:

Philosopher: I have been thinking of the pocopo.
Fool: So have I. What is it?
Philosopher: The pocopo is a small Brazilian animal chiefly remarkable for the singularity of its diet. A pocopo eats nothing but other pocopos. As these are not easily obtained, the animal mortality from starvation is very great. As a result, there are fewer mouths to feed, and by consequence, the race is rapidly multiplying.
Fool: From whom had you this?

80

Philosopher: A professor of political economy.
Fool: Let us rise and uncover.

The pulling and the hauling of conflicting panaceas in Washington hardly touched our economic lives. No siren, hooting its dread, warned us to take cover.

But I began to notice that the string of contractors that had queued up at the desk of Mr. Evans, the estimator, was not quite as long nor as insistent as it had been when I first became secretary of Wheeler Osgood Millwork Company. It was not the buyer, now, who was importunate. The pathway to our door led out as well as in, and I found myself treading the pathway to the door of the buyer.

"There's business to be had," said Mr. Wheeler. "Go after it."

I learned what it meant to be a city salesman. I went after business. I tramped through the half-cleared outskirts of the town looking for orders. Whenever I saw a load of cedar that looked like foundation sills, I followed it and barged in to corral the contract for the doors and windows, cresting and spindles. In all innocence, still, I pinned my faith to the future of spindles.

From time to time, I called on Mr. Goss, the contractor, in the hope that this time he would give me the order for all that millwork for the Tourist Hotel. Goss always found an excuse for keeping me waiting. The Northern Pacific, he said, wasn't quite ready to jingle the bell for full steam ahead. "Some of those Wall Street fellows," he said, "are kinda holding things up. But don't worry," he said; "it'll be all right — mebbe next week."

Eastern money. It had poured into the Puget Sound country like a flood. The source, we had thought, was an ever-welling spring that could not go dry. But now the flood was receding, and we paid no heed. Like a creeping paralysis, the forces that play such havoc with our national life were finding their way into our West Coast concerns, but we still built our confidence on the shifting sands of Northern Pacific promises.

Carrol D. Wright, the first United States Commissioner of Labor, had made his initial annual report:

> Industry has been enormously developed, cities have been transformed, distances covered, and a new set of economic tools have been given to rich countries, and in a more reasonable amount, to

poorer ones. What is strictly necessary has been done, oftentimes to superfluity. This full supply of economic tools, to meet the wants of nearly all the branches of commerce and industry, is the most important factor in the present industrial depression. It is true that the discovery of new processes of manufacture will undoubtedly continue, but it will not leave room for marked extension, such as has been witnessed during the last fifty years, or afford remunerative employment of the vast amount of capital which has been created during that period. . . . The day of large profits is probably past. There may be room for further intensive, but not extensive, development of industry in the present area of civilization. . . . Supplying themselves with the full facilities for industry and commerce will give to each great nation of Europe and America something to do, but the part of each in this work will be small, and far from large enough to insure more than a temporary activity.

Thus spoke the Jeremiah of the East in the early 1890's. I showed the clipping to Mr. Wheeler.

"Pooh," he said. "Read this." He unfolded the morning *Ledger.*

Industrially, this nation has been especially blessed. It has taken its place at the head of affairs. It has awakened to a sense of its strength to enhance prosperity. It is at peace with every other power. There is not even a threat of strife. Within its borders, capital and labour work well in amity. If the rich have become richer, it is because of the creation of wealth, and in this, the poor share. They are not becoming poorer. Invention has been notable. The new year is greeted by millions, smiling at the dawn.

But the dawn lay in the East, and it was in the East that the storm was gathering. The great era of railroad expansion was drawing to its close, and the new dawn was ushering in the day of receiverships.

I was wandering about the terrace of the Tacoma Hotel, hopeful still, when I met my old Yale contemporary, Marshall Bond. Marshall had just come back from the East, where he had been gathering all the news from the big outside world.

"How's things, Marshall?" I asked.

Fresh from the seat of trouble, Marshall looked doubtful.

"Not so good," said Marshall. "It's those farmers. They've organized the Populist Party. Seems they want everything free: free silver, free banking laws; everything free, grub, lodging, clothes, I s'pose."

"But what's that got to do with Tacoma?"

"Plenty," said Marshall. "They're attacking the very foundation of society, the rights of property, everything." And Marshall said we had something called "credit inflation," and a fellow in Wall Street said it was caused by what he called a pleth-o-ra of money, and you couldn't get any money when you wanted it, and Wall Street was pretty scared. It was my first experience with words like these and it sounded ominous. I repeated them to Mr. Wheeler.

"It's just a little recession," Mr. Wheeler assured me. "Don't worry."

And I didn't worry. We were still a little cosmos, whirling in our own orbit; and if the bigger outside world was jumping its smooth track of prosperity, it wouldn't collide with us as long as the Union Pacific continued to push a second right of way to our door. William Allen White, back in Emporia, could write, "What's the matter with Kansas," and we could read it with a pitying smile. If the Kansas farmers could not get enough for their corn to pay for the cost of raising it, the unhappy fact touched our minds and hearts very much as did the stories of hunger in Poland. Anyway, the magic wand of Congress could be waved again, and we would all be happy.

83

CHAPTER XIII

"TRULY, THERE IS A TIDE in the affairs of men; but there is no gulf stream, setting forever in one direction." The tide was ebbing, but one never notes the turn of the tide until its outward flow becomes strong. We had a grand free ride on the flowing tide to fortune. Now the surfboard had dumped us on the beach, and all hands scrambled to find a toehold against the undertow that tugged at our feet to drag us out to sea again.

But we were in the morning of life, and in the bright lexicon of youth, we just couldn't find the word "fail." The *Ledger* greeted the next New Year's Day with its regular editorial paean of confidence, this time tempered with modesty:

> A whole year ahead and no mistakes made yet. The time is propitious to take our bearings, make our plans and start on the right foot.
>
> A great many people devote New Year's Day to good resolutions. They swear off. They quit smoking, or chewing, or lying, or stealing — or they think they do. And they put in the day in an excess of indulgence, just to get a good start. They punish themselves for a week or two by refraining from their pet vices, or virtues, as the case may be, and then fall back into their old way and their last state is worse than their first. It has been proved by actual experience that New Year's Day reformation, in the way of swearing off, is a dismal failure.
>
> Suppose we swear *on* something. There are a number of things that need attention of this kind; for instance:
>
> Tacoma has very quietly but very certainly stepped forward to second place as a wheat exporting place, on this coast, but we are in the race for first and can win if we want to. We have not provided the ships with the buoys they need, and we have left them without proper defense in case of fire. Suppose we swear *on* that we will attend to this important matter at once.

Faint hearts were bucked up by the following, set in large type:

STATISTICS

TACOMA'S SOLID PROGRESS DURING THE YEAR JUST PAST! FIGURES AND FACTS THAT GIVE THE LIE TO THE CROAKERS! CITY OF DESTINY FLOURISHING IN SPITE OF HARD TIMES! MANUFACTURIES AND INDUSTRIES GROWING AND THRIVING! THE NEW YEAR PROMISES TO BE MORE PROSPEROUS THAN THE OLD!

It was not a show of the valor of ignorance. It was a display of a quiet courage that declined to count the odds against us; a cheerful acceptance of the challenge to turn the ebbing tide into a new flood.

On another page was the lighthearted advertisement of Abe Gross's brick store:

> A SPECIAL DISPATCH has been handed us by the weather maker, and they claim that a hurricane, far more severe than the CYCLONE which passed through our store last year, will visit each and every department of our store. HURRICANE SALE!
>
> The prices during the sale will be nothing compared to the CYCLONE SALE of last year.

"We had a good dance," Abe said, as he grinned; "Now the damn fiddler is passing his hat."

The yellowed pages of that old *Ledger* recall a period when American youth accepted the dubbing it got for the follies it had committed. We were entering a depression in that small world on Puget Sound, the like of which I have not seen since, and, as the morass got deeper, we conceived the innocent idea that only hard work could pull us out of the slough. And we worked, hard, ten hours a day and six days a week — the day of rest dedicated to plans for meeting next week's payroll. We didn't beat our collective breast; instead, we tightened our collective belt. Nobody invented a new vocabulary of phrases with which, handily, to cast the blame for our predicament onto the shoulders of some, higher up in the economic scale, who had not perhaps danced quite so wildly.

But we had reached only the edge of the quicksands, and we felt our way, looking for hillocks of firm ground. Our eyes were fixed on the other side, sure that a long breath and a few long jumps would land us on solid earth and good footing. We couldn't know how wide and long the morass was.

I say "we," for the same compulsion held us all in its grip, in the factory as in the office. The men in the factory worked hard, not in fear of being fired for some whim in the office, but because they knew, as we in the office knew, that the paycheck came, not as manna from heaven, but from the honest work of a smooth-functioning whole. We were no heroes of a western movie. We were just a crew of young men, drawn together in the common purpose to "grow up with the country" to full stature as independent citizens of a happy town, which itself would grow as we worked.

It was a grand crew that worked in the factory. Louis, our yard foreman, who kept bachelor independence afloat in a shack-boat, rising and falling with the tide in the waterway under the bridge, taught me more philosophy than I had learned in college. Louis read Rousseau and Voltaire and other fathers of modern thought. I think he must have read Thoreau, too, for Walden Pond never gave the sage more complete escape than his leaky shack gave Louis.

"Own dis business?" asked Louis.

"Yes, a piece of it."

"Ay tank you wrong," said Louis. "Ay tank dis business own *you*. You sit in office all day makin' figures. Hard work. Bimeby super come an' say, 'We got to have new automatic trim saw,' and you gotta buy. You gotta make paycheck for me. Then come alwiss tax feller to take what's left. Me, I got no business an' no business own me. When I die, no trouble. When you die, you got a lot of machines, ain't it?"

Fresh from Vermont, where the native Yankee tongue was still the recognized language of the country, I was fascinated by the infinite variety of men in the factory. Their personal and racial idiosyncrasies were as varied as their accents. There were "stickers" and "short-stakers." A "sticker" is one who sticks to his job, making slow but sure progress toward the higher and more responsible levels. The "short-staker," bored to desperation with monotony, jumps from job to job like Kipling's Tramp Royal.

Gus was a sticker. We used to say he was foaled in the factory. At the legal age, he began wheeling shavings to the boiler room, studying meanwhile to find a better way of moving the shavings. Of course he found it. Following the precepts of Sir Joseph Porter:

"He handled those shavings so careful-ee
That he soon became the super of the factor-ee."

Rising to the position of superintendent, Gus became an expert on power transmission. He spent hours explaining to me why a little pulley driven by a big pulley made things go faster. To him the hum of the cutter head was like the music of the spheres. And between discussion of the merits of a rope versus a belt, Gus, son of a German-born father, told me much that I hadn't learned in college of the duties as well as perquisites of American citizenship.

"Look," said Gus, "at what Uncle Sam has done for me. I owe him the best licks I can put in."

Gus discharged his full duty to Uncle Sam. In time he graduated, *cum laude,* to the full stature of a good and honest businessman. He came to have a business of his own, or at least he called it his own. He was shackled to the desk of a wood-working business that owned him. Like any good businessman, he wore his shackles with fortitude.

Joe was a short-staker. Throughout the winter months he worked stubbornly at his job, earning his pay and saving it for his one supreme purpose: to taste the spice of life, which is variety. As the gray skies of winter broke and the rains changed to the mists of spring, Joe began to take on the look of a mystic, in touch with the reality that lay beyond the surface consciousness. He struggled against the thing that was tugging at him, but his struggles went weaker and weaker. The thing was stronger than all the moral concepts put together. The boys said he took to writing poetry.

"But, by God," said his teammate, "if he did, he kep' it to hisself."

Then one fine day the morning whistle failed to bring Joe to his overall locker. He was off to try his hand at new jobs in new places. His pay was good and he had earned it,

> But that's no reason man should labour all 'is life on one same shift; life's none so long.

Was it weakness that Joe couldn't stick to his job? Or was it the fine courage to claim his freedom? Would it be traitorous to the employer class if I acknowledge an understanding sympathy with Joe? I suppose so, but I must risk the imputation of treachery. One part of me rambled about the world with Joe.

Green was black, very black. Soft of speech, he had the look of gentle patience that his race inherited through long years of service. Green tended no machine, piled no lumber, shoveled no shavings;

so, when wanted, he couldn't be found at any particular spot. He was just somewhere around. Armed with a big tin washtub, he rambled about doing what he called "tidyin' up." If a water closet failed to gurgle when you pulled the chain, someone called, "Where's Green?" and "Where's Green?" went echoing through the plant from mouth to mouth.

"Yassuh, yassuh. I fix'm," said Green, and he straightway called the engineer, a most efficient disposition of the problem.

At intervals, Green would come to my desk with his most engaging smile (and Green's smile was engaging enough to melt the heart of a dictator — which I was not), and, he would say, "Mist' Ripley, ah wants to trans-ack a lil bisness with you."

"Yes, Green; want a raise?"

"Oh, no, suh. Ah don't need no raise. As jes wants to loan five dollahs from you."

"All right, Green. I'll borrow five dollars to you," and I handed him the gold piece.

When Green said business, he meant business. It might be six months after the deal that the bookkeeper would hand me a pocketful of nickels and dimes amounting to exactly five dollars, which had been paid in by Green at such time as he could manage it, with the injunction: "You give this to Mist' Ripley. Don't say nothin'; he'll understand."

Loyal friends, these men, honest, brave, and intelligent, each putting his back and head into the job of bettering his condition, as I, in the office, was trying, less effectively, to better mine. The chief difference between us lay in the fact that they knew their jobs better than I knew mine.

CHAPTER XIV

FATHER SAT IN THE DIRECTORS' ROOM of the Rutland County National Bank, his fishing tackle spread out on the black walnut directors' table, his mind divided between fish and fear of the coming panic. From the panic of '73, which followed the Civil War, he recalled such phrases as "unlimited credit," "reckless speculation," and "over-expansion." The words "unlimited credit" brought to mind the note of his fiddler-son out in Tacoma, endorsed by himself. The note lay among the assets of the bank, coming to light at each directors' meeting.

John Miller, also a director, made it his job to ramble about among the farmers who asked for credit, taking a look at the fences and farm machinery, casting an appraising eye at the swill pail and, particularly, at the woodpile, as a basis for credit.

"General," John said at a meeting of directors, "a guitar, a song, and a willing heart ain't really good collateral. Better get out there and kinda look into that Wheeler Osgood business. Look at their lumber piles, and see if they've got their storm windows up yet. Looks like winter's coming."

"Well, John," said Father, "I believe you're right. The salmon will be running now, and the trout season is on. It's time I went."

He packed his bag and, more solicitously, his Orvis trout rod, his salmon rod, and all the bright colored feathers he could extract from Mother's bonnets — for Father's chief rule in life was "When in doubt, go fishing." He made his own flies, which, he maintained, were infinitely better than the hackles and coachmen he could buy. Thus equipped, he left for Puget Sound.

Father couldn't abide the thought of trolling for salmon. No salmon in Puget Sound had ever been known to rise to a fly, but that, he said was because the Puget Sound salmon had never been trained by a real fly-fisherman. You had to know the mind of a salmon, he said, as he learned to know it on the roaring Restigouche. Those murderous trollers out there fished for food, damn 'em. He would show the pot-fishermen what a sportsman could do with a fly, once you got on proper terms with a salmon. Phantom minnows, indeed! A salmon has some respect for a fly, if you know how to cast.

Father, all his life, had been the Rock of Ages to which his numerous and extensive family clung in stormy weather. We hailed his coming, like marooned sailors, and the company lost no time in getting a toehold on the rock.

As I brought Father into the office, Mr. Wheeler was opening the morning's mail, thriftily slitting the envelopes all around and saving them for memorandum pads, bound together on a bit of shingle with a rubber band.

"Waste not, want not," said Mr. Wheeler as he turned to greet us.

"That's good," said Father. "I take it you want not, then, with all those unwasted envelopes."

In the way of Rutland banking, Father looked at the lumber piles. They looked pretty dejected. He looked at the accounts receivable. Most of them were hoary with age. He looked at all the liabilities.

"The liabilities," said Mr. Wheeler, "are all right. When those notes for lumber we've bought come due, I just get 'em extended. When we buy lumber, we get the price settled first; then *I* settle the terms." Trade was a little slow, he said, but that was only seasonal. "What we've got to do," said Mr. Wheeler, "is to reach out and lead."

"Lead what? — and where?" Father asked.

"Now, General," said Mr. Wheeler, "that's no way to talk. Lead everywhere. This is no boomtown; we have now a solid, substantial growth. We've got the Northern Pacific behind us, and the Union Pacific is grading its right of way to our doors. And we're the Gateway to the Orient, too. There's China, with her teeming millions, and Japan, where they live in paper houses. They need our doors." He pulled out a drawer and showed Father an inquiry that had come, through the Congregational Church, from a missionary. The missionary wanted to buy six doors, if the price was right, and a bathtub, which was not in our line but on which we might make a small profit. It was our prize exhibit.

Mr. Wheeler, untaught in psychology and innocent of self-analysis, was a first class extrovert, pinning his faith to the word as taught by the Congregational Church. "Knock, and it shall be opened unto you" epitomized his simple creed. He proceeded to knock. "All we need," said Mr. Wheeler, "is a little more capital; what you might call a permanent loan."

"Something new and original in banking practice," said Father.

"Oh," said Mr. Wheeler, "the interest would be paid regularly and promptly, of course. That kind of loan would make us free to reach out and lead. Tacoma's prosperity has been so great that our local banks are short of ready capital to make such loans, but wouldn't it be a fine thing for the Rutland County National to reach out and lead in our West Coast development?" Mr. Wheeler was a bit breathless. "That's about it, isn't it, Tom?"

"That's about it," I said.

Father lighted a cigar and reached for his hat. "Trout are biting now, anyway," he said. "Come on, Tom, we'll find Mr. Morrill and try Chambers Creek."

Mr. Morrill kept a book shop; he sold stationery and pictures of Mount Tacoma. And you could get in his shop the few books that the publisher's agents had pushed over on him, including several copies of *Robert Elsmere* and a reprint of *The Rise of Silas Lapham*. It was a jolly sort of store, for Mr. Morrill was always ready to drop literary talk for a little fishing chat. As we came in, he dropped a half-sold customer to greet us, his face alight.

"Don't let us interrupt you," said Father.

"Doesn't matter in the least," said Mr. Morrill.

"Chamber's Creek all fished out yet by those bait fishermen?" asked Father.

"Can't tell till you try," said Mr. Morrill.

"Try when?" asked Father. He thought of the motto on my desk. "Do it now," he said.

That fishing day on Chamber's Creek stands marked as though by a signpost at the fork in the road I travel in memory. We drove in Mr. Morrill's carryall through little wisps of misty rain to a spot where the horse would stand hitched. The mists cleared and golden shafts of sunshine pierced them as we jointed our rods and began whipping upstream through the tangle of lovely vegetation that only the moist Puget Sound country can produce. The trout, hungry and gamy, broke water at each cast. What mattered it that customers were reluctant and creditors importunate? "I have laid aside business and gone a-fishing."

Where the stream tumbled through the bank of ferns into a foamy pool, Father straightened his leader and whipped out his line with the graceful skill that he of all fishermen could command, all set for a difficult cast. The line tautened, the reel whirring as it paid out, and the cast hung.

"Dammit," said Father, "I'm snagged."

He clambered up the bank to find his homemade brown hackle caught in a most unlikely thing, a little square white post with letters painted on it.

"Look, Morrill," he called. "I'm snagged on a curious thing. How in the world did that little white post get there?"

Mr. Morrill, whipping away in the riffles upstream, reeled in and waded down to have a look. "Oh, that," said he, "that's the corner of Two Hundred and Forty-eighth Street and Sunset Boulevard."

Father sat down on a fallen cedar, the better to let the intelligence sink in. "Mr. Morrill," he said, "don't tell me, in all seriousness, that you have streets surveyed way out here in this wilderness."

"General," said Mr. Morrill, "can't you eastern fellows realize that this town is going to be as big as London — and soon, too?"

Father could quote Scripture as readily as he could Shakespeare.

"The city was large and great, but the people were few therein, and the houses were not builded."

Father would have made an intriguing subject for a psychologist. He was, at heart, a sentimentalist. He carefully cultivated a hard exterior to match the granite Vermont hills, but, in spite of his pose, a vein of the romantic would push through like an outcropping of gold-bearing ore between the rugged boulders of character. And always the romantic vision centered on the good fight for a just cause, the fight with your back against the wall.

After a good day's fishing, Mr. Morrill's fantastic vision, Mr. Wheeler's airy confidence, and my own ill-judged enthusiasm worked together to shape his decision. Here were men who were following the cosmic law of creation: converting the unused wilderness to human use. Somewhere men and women were needing the things created by this small mill. So much work and worry were entitled to just compensation. The laborer was worthy of his hire. We struck while the iron was hot and Father capitulated. Once more he endorsed a note to the Rutland County National Bank.

"Gentlemen," he said to us, "you have not yet begun to fight. You will stay on the bridge of this ship till she sinks."

The Trader's Bank in Tacoma had a private office for Mr. Fitch, its president. It always bucked me up to read of its splendors as depicted by the *Ledger*:

> The private offices of the president and cashier are enclosed by parallel partitions of *natural mahogany*, this wood being used wherever wood is required throughout the entire room. Surmounting the woodwork of the private offices are delicately wrought panels of cathedral glass, each with a center composed of a wreath of amber-tinted glass. Surmounting the marble rail which forms the front of the counter, the grace and artistic designs of the metal worker have deftly wrought the yielding Japanese copper into winsome effect.

To this shrine of finance, the executive board of Wheeler Osgood hotfooted it with our note. Mr. Fitch sat under the amber-tinted glass, girding himself to refuse us more credit. He hardened his heart and set his lips for a "no." We flashed the note. He fairly grabbed at it.

"New capital!" he boomed. "That's what this country needs — new capital!"

Mr. Osgood, our vice-president, had spent his youth in Vermont, and Vermont principle continued to guide his course. He remembered Eli Brigg's rule: "When you're gittin', git plenty."

"Doesn't this increase in capital assets entitle us to a further line of credit?" he asked.

"Why, yes, I suppose it does, now I come to think of it. How much?"

"How much have you got?" asked Mr. Wheeler.

We got the limit. Taking our cue from Mr. Fitch, we called it new capital, undismayed by the thought of the new liabilities that must be entered on the other side of the ledger. With the light hearts of the reprieved, we went back to the mill to draw checks for the next payday, which was dangerously near.

CHAPTER XV

Dᴜʀɪɴɢ ᴀʟʟ ᴛʜɪs ᴛɪᴍᴇ Seattle, with a perversity that baffled me, kept on growing. With all the padding of the census that we could devise, Tacoma could never quite overtake her. Racing along in the zest for population, just about neck and neck during the lean years, in some nefarious way she kept showing her heels. And she was plumb obstinate about the name of the mountain.

"Darn 'em," said Ike Striker; "they keep calling the mountain 'Rainier.' I s'pose it's because it's rainier up there than 'tis down here." The ancient wheeze never failed to get Ike the laugh that he expected.

But you couldn't laugh off those census-taker fellows with their sharp pencils. Something had to be done to settle this *querelle des choches* and put Seattle where she belonged — in second place. Seattle wasn't the terminus of anything; her hills were much steeper than ours; and she hadn't anything like our "natural facilities." But she had an uncomfortable way of utilizing what she had, while her go-getters said of ours: "Their facilities are still 'natural'." Something had to be done, and cooperation was the word.

We were natural joiners in Tacoma. The town rejoiced in clubs, organization, and every form of cooperative effort. We had a Chamber of Commerce, very dignified indeed, with a membership composed of the captains of industry who could best afford to pay the rent. We had a Commercial Club, less exclusive, open to most of those who could pay for their lunches. And we had the Union Club, the University Club, and the whole gamut of ladies' clubs, musical and literary. But all this cooperation was not enough. We needed a Boosters' Club. We organized one to take in every civic-minded man who believed in its motto: "Boost! Don't knock!" I joined, of course.

The Boosters met and debated long and seriously over the adoption of a slogan. We believed in the power of slogans.

"City of Destiny," I proposed.

"No, that's old stuff." I was voted down.

94

"'Tacoma, the Gateway.' Now, how's that? Short and snappy."

Frank Cole, the wisecracker, saw the catch. "In a week's time Seattle'll be hollering 'Tacoma get-a-way.' 'Twon't do."

Louis Pratt spoke. "Something gentle, persuasive, but at the same time, confident. What about 'You'll *like* Tacoma'?"

We pondered that. "Folks'd think it's something to eat — like Heinz's pork and beans," Frank predicted.

"Watch Tacoma Grow!" shouted Brewer.

"Watch Tacoma Grow! Watch Tacoma Grow!" roared the Boosters. It went over big.

The battle cry was printed on stickers and pasted by baggage-smashers on all outgoing trains. It was put up in all shop windows. Seattle and Portland were littered with dodgers carrying the slogan.

After resolving this momentous question, the chairman posed a question which we received more soberly: "Now that you're all set to watch Tacoma grow, what are you going to do about it? Sit on a fence and watch it grow?"

We hadn't thought of that. Somehow we thought that a slogan, repeated often enough and loudly enough, would turn the trick. The chairman insisted that we must make Tacoma grow: not only in number, but in the character of its citizens; not only in the area of its business section, but in the grace and beauty of its homes; not only in the number of its homes, but in the neat greenery of the vacant lots between the homes. And we must not forget the meaning of the word "Booster." It meant giving a leg up to the fellow who needed it.

The Boosters felt the pricking of a new sensation in the cardiac region as they listened.

"If you own a vacant lot and want to sell it for what it's worth, make it look like a good place to live. Clean it up; plant some flowers and, God knows we need 'em, some trees — with leaves on 'em instead of needles. And if you don't own a vacant lot, walk past some other fellow's lot and carry off a tin can or two. Never walk the streets of this city of ours without leaving it a little better for your passing."

Billy Trowbridge and I left the meeting with swelling hearts, prepared to make a lovesome spot of a vacant lot. I can't honestly say that we made it more lovesome for our passing, but we made a beginning.

95

"Greatly begin, though thou hast time but for a can," paraphrased Billy. We each gathered a tin can out of a lot and walked down the street with them, feeling as foolish as we looked.

But Ike Striker, the literal-minded "common man," put in evenings at his vacant lot. He grubbed it, he hoed it, he planted flowers according to his light, and he planted a rose hedge along the street side. The slogan was no opiate to Ike's conscience.

St. Peter's Church, built in 1873, "stood among its shack brethren smack up against Tacoma's last remnant of God's first temples—a mammoth fir trunk that formed the tower for the clanging bell on its sawed-off top.... If I could have counted the ring growth record of its years, I would have found that the living bell tower had stood there, defying the buffetings of Puget Sound storms... perhaps before the devoted monks placed the stones of Glastonbury Abbey."

"It was a wooden city I looked out upon... with the forest which gave it birth still keeping its inviolate secrets, its greenery pressing in from all sides, but with no blade of green within." Above, a winter scene of the wooden city's principal residential district, looking northwest to the Olympic Mountains. Below, a fancy, and somewhat fanciful — birds-eye view captures in loving detail all the orderly bustle and progress so fulsomely promoted by the boomers.

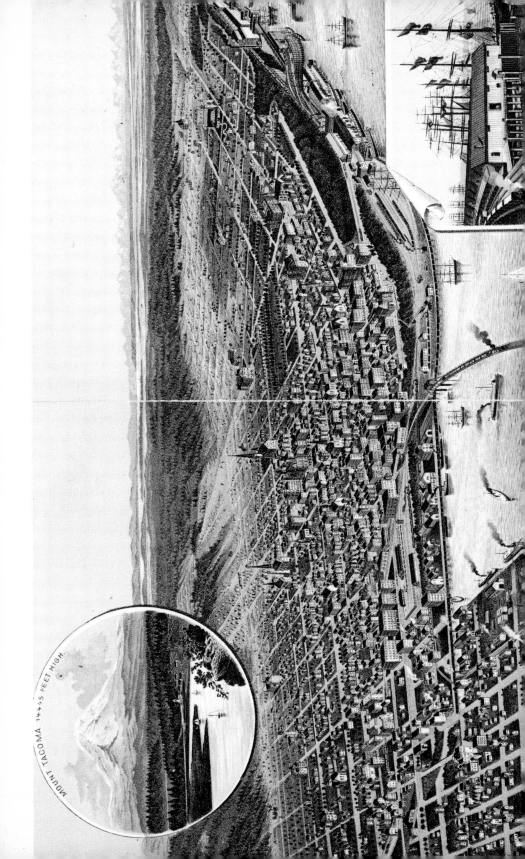

MOUNT TACOMA 14445 FEET HIGH.

With the completion of the Northern Pacific's mighty switch-back through the Cascades (right), "the morning of life dawned again. Again the new town cut loose and capered. They hauled out the old gun—armament of a Russian gunboat which had come with the purchase of Alaska in 1867—and they rammed it and they rammed it; and they fired it and they fired it till it was too hot to fire. Then they took a drink and they took another and they fired it again." Above, snow blankets the railroad's Half Moon Yards at the foot of the town.

"The commerce of the world, passing and re-passing in endless pageant at our feet!" Above, the mill dock stacks lumber for the holds of waiting ships. Below, "We include in our count the fleet of Siwash canoes, loaded to the gunwales with mixed families of braves, klootch-mans, and papooses. Singing to the rhythmic beat of their paddles, from the outer world of the reservation they come for the hop-picking. With a mighty splash, they ground the big dug-out canoes on the mud flats near the warehouse and within sound of the hiu-chick-chick of the railroad. They throw out blankets, bark, baskets, blackjack, and babies in one riot of color and strong smells, and set up their cozy housekeeping in the ooze of the tide flats."

The Tacoma Hotel, designed by Stanford White and described, American fashion, as "the two-hundred-and-sixty-seven-thousand-dollar hotel." Furniture was imported from Wanamaker's, and waiters from Philadelphia. Its opening was one of the town's grandest affairs: "Seattle and Portland had been watching, waiting, counting the days. Envy and curiosity lured the rivals to the grand opening. They strolled about the spacious lobby, practicing the feel of hotel habitués.... From the bar, which was finished first, to the yet-unfinished top story, the place was packed. The widespread lobby echoed to the sound of dancing feet and the voices of speculators in corner lots, predicting, predicting, predicting."

At right, the home of C. L. Dewey.

Cascade Steam Laundry.

"TACOMA'S SOLID PROGRESS!
FIGURES AND FACTS THAT GIVE THE LIE TO THE CROAKERS!
CITY OF DESTINY FLOURISHING IN SPITE OF HARD TIMES!
MANUFACTURIES AND INDUSTRIES GROWING AND THRIVING!

"It was not a show of the valor of ignorance. It was a display of a quiet courage that declined to count the odds against us; a cheerful acceptance of the challenge to turn the ebbing tide into a new flood."

Mason and Finley: Coffee Dealers.

Enterprise given substance: Chamber of Commerce Building, Pacific Avenue.

The worldly and the unworldly: the Tacoma Wall Paper Co., and in the background, the Presbyterian Church.

Fire insurance, homeopathy, and fluid assets: 10th Street and Pacific Avenue. In the right background, the Tacoma Hotel.

At left, the headquarters building of the Northern Pacific Railroad. Right center, the Tacoma Hotel.

The Tacoma Mill Company's Railroad Days float. The town was ever ready to celebrate everything and anything—particularly its own entrepreneurial virtues. But—"We were entering a depression in that small world on Puget Sound, the like of which I have not seen since, and, as the morass got deeper, we conceived the innocent idea that only hard work could pull us out of the slough. . . . But we had reached only the edge of the quicksands, and we felt our way, looking for hillocks of firm ground. We couldn't know how wide and long the morass was. . . ."

CHAPTER XVI

A SLOGAN WAS NOT ENOUGH. Brave words could not reverse the tide that was ebbing. The great London House of Baring collapsed and joggled the economic structure of the whole world. Like a pile of jackstraws, delicately balanced, the whole thing shivered, cracked, and fell apart. New York shook with the jolt and passed the jitters westward to Chicago, to St. Paul, on across the prairies over the Rockies, the Cascades, the shocks becoming more severe as they reached us, who were the least able to stand them. London drew on New York, and New York drew on the Puget Sound country. We had borrowed up to the limit — and beyond. Now payday, which had seemed so distant, was upon us.

The panic began with whispers: "They say the Merchant's National won't open tomorrow."

The Merchant's did open, but, at the same moment, a demand for the Merchant's money came from New York and the bank closed.

"They say!" "They say!"

"How 'bout Traders? They say 82 per cent of the deposits have been withdrawn."

"Aw, don't worry. Directors have gone to New York. They'll get a truck load o' money there."

And they did. The bank struggled valiantly for a few days, paying out to the last copper cent until it closed its door in the face of a long line of desperate men.

"They say the Tacoma National's goin' to close."

"Naw, they ain't. Blackwell's raised seventy thousand dollars on his own and put it in."

Blackwell did, but the earth continued to heave and the bank crashed.

I began to learn something of the meaning of the words "liquid assets." Such assets as I had were so very liquid that I couldn't hold them. They trickled out almost before they reached my pocket. Drawing my salary was about as painful as extracting a tooth.

There was always a payday just ahead, and on payday you couldn't hand out promises to men who had done their work well and faithfully. They came to the window in hope and in confidence. That was one obligation that must be met though not a nickel was left in the till after payment. I envied the man who could draw his meager wages in cash and carry it home to his wife. He was secure — for a week at least.

I took stock of our assets. Charlotte and I owned some boom-style furniture bought at boom prices, but the furniture, though paid for, was not "liquid." And Charlotte owned that lot in Mason's Addition, bought nearly three years earlier under the stimulus of Allen C. Mason's advertising. Attached to the deed was Mr. Mason's promise that, if the purchaser was not satisfied with his bargain after three years, Mr. Mason would buy the lot back again at the purchase price plus 9 per cent interest, compounded semiannually. We had a tin box in which this, which was to be the foundation of our fortunes, had lain exactly two years, eleven months, and fifteen days. I wondered, was this "liquid capital"? I took the precious document and hurried to Mr. Mason's office. I rehearsed my "it's only that I need the money" speech, but I might have spared myself any apprehension.

Mr. Mason sat at his desk, watching the ebb tide of his fortunes with the same indifference with which he had watched its flood. He was dictating to Lizzie Harrington: "Owing to a temporary depression, amounting almost to paralysis." He looked up. "That's all, Miss Harrington." A bit shamefaced, I presented the document.

Mr. Mason was a game gentleman. He never gave me a reproachful glance. "Mr. Hopping," he roared, "bring me contract number so and so, in the name of Charlotte H. Clement," and with not a quaver in his voice, "a check for three hundred dollars plus interest at 9 per cent compounded semiannually, for two years, eleven months, and fifteen days." There was no pleading for delay, no pointing out the future value of the lot. The redemption of the contract was done with the gallant gesture of a Cyrano de Bergerac. Mr. Hopping drew the check, and I escaped, feeling like the piker I was. As I left, I heard Mr. Mason resuming his dictation ". . . owing to a temporary depression amounting almost to paralysis . . ." (Lizzie afterwards confided to me that she longed for a typewriter that would type that entire sentence with one stroke of a single key, so often had she had to spell it out on her old Blickensdorfer.)

To the young businessman from Vermont, the interview provided a lesson in the art of taking it on the chin, gracefully. I have many times wished we had kept that lovely bit of land as a memento of those days of bitter medicine, taken without a yelp. Instead, I deposited the money in a bank that exploded in my face the next week.

Allen C. Mason was already a legendary hero when I came to Tacoma. A decade earlier he had selected the town of planked roads and trails through the forest as the city of his vision. As the story went, he settled his family in a three-room house, paid the rent in advance, and then counted the handful of silver left in his pant's pocket. It came to two dollars and eighty-five cents. He invested in gilt paper from which he cut letters, to paste on the transom of his office-home. The letters read:

ALLEN C. MASON
REAL ESTATE

The gilt paper had cost thirty-five cents, leaving two dollars and a half in his pocket. By some magic of geometric progression he transmuted this capital into five dollars. Again he waved his wand and it became ten dollars. He was on his pyrotechnic way.

A dreamer was Mr. Mason. He dreamed the dreams on which the things of substance arise. He was a doer, too, and in an incredibly short time, he turned from his dream to the instant need of bridges to span the deep, green-clad gulches that crossed the path to Mason's Addition. The bridges carried timber, brick, and stone for the building of a library, which he planned as the cultural center of his dream acres.

The bridges carried also the ecstasies of hand-sawed ornament for the turreted castle home that he built to signalize his faith in his dream. And they carried the hope and confidence of men and women who followed his light and bought bits of that green and happy land, "overlooking the waters of Puget Sound" and not forgetting "a glimpse of majestic Mount Tacoma."

Faith and works marched hand in hand to a meteoric but brief success. Happily he watched his mounting bank balance, but he saw it only as the measure of the fulfillment of his dreams. His religion was faith and hope for a better and better Tacoma. In that day of passion for crowded population, that meant, of course, a bigger and bigger Tacoma.

But now Mason, whose bright dream had led me to Tacoma, was wiped out. Crash followed crash, shattering the dream. As a bank toppled, it fell over on to its neighbor, bringing it, too, down to ruin. London, though shaken, was still solvent, so the banks with British names — the London and San Francisco and the Bank of British Columbia — stood the strain; and Chester Thorne, with the courage of youth, saved the National Bank of Commerce by engaging his whole private fortune in the struggle. When the wreckage was cleared away, Ike Striker voiced the confidence of the town amid the ruins. "By golly," he said, "we've saved 10 per cent of the banks anyway."

Mr. Mason, walking down Pacific Avenue, looked at his gold watch. It was lunchtime, but the price of a lunch was now a matter for consideration. "A gold watch!" said Mr. Mason. "Now what am I doing with a gold watch when I can't pay the rent?" He stepped into Richard Vaeth's jewelry store and asked how much the gold case was worth. Twenty dollars, he was told. And how much would it cost to put the works into a nickel one? It would cost two dollars and a half.

"Shift it," said Mr. Mason. "That'll be a start on my liquidation."

The crash winnowed out the crooked and the fainthearted from the honest and courageous. Paul Schulze, he who as land agent for the Northern Pacific had cut so wide a swath in the little financial and social world, was tipped off that a bunch of auditors, those nosy fellows with sharp pencils, were coming out to investigate his affairs. He lived royally on Yakima Avenue in the center of the socially elect, where he scattered largesse with the generosity and noble disregard of consequences generally displayed with other people's money. And he kept another establishment, more modest but none the less *recherché*, where he installed Marie Wainwright, the actress with whom, it was said, he was about to commit matrimony. She dazzled us as she drove about in the spiffiest of his carriages.

Paul Schulze chose between disgrace and oblivion. "Kono," he said to his Japanese butler, "I go away on a long journey." He opened a last bottle of champagne. He wrote a goodbye letter to Marie. He took the ready revolver from his desk drawer and left the auditors to enjoy their investigations. They found him in the big room where the smart set of the town had been so riotously entertained. His funeral was described as "quite magnificent."

There were other murky displays. Smoke mingled with bits of charred paper, poured from the chimneys of some of the commercial houses, as telltale evidence of a casual sort of bookkeeping went up in smoke and down again, weighted by the drizzle of Puget Sound mist. It was "the cold grey dawn of the morning after." The chink of twenty-dollar gold pieces was no longer heard in the pockets of the traders. Nickels and dimes made music so soft that it was scarcely heard, because there were so few of them to jingle. The high bridges spanning the gulches made handy jumping-off places, and the deep ferns hid the remains of some of the discouraged revelers of yesterday.

The party was over.

CHAPTER XVII

WHEN ANYBODY STARTS TO TALK ABOUT the 1929-32 depression, I chip in and do a bit of boasting. I tell them about a depression that *was* a depression. It is the habit of the old-timers, I know. Old soldiers always claim the stage. "Speaking of battles," they begin, and the evening is dead for all but the old soldier. If an incautious young-ster ventures the tale of a blizzard, the old-timer will leap into the middle of the circle. "What do you know about blizzards? Now in the blizzard of '88, the snow was piled clear up to the second story windows on Chapel Street — etc., etc." If the youngster is wise, he will quickly retire before the old blizzard expert.

If anyone of the lost generation wants to match depressions with me, I'm ready to take him on. I'll tell him about *my* depression. "Bank holiday," I'll say it was a bank holiday, that one of mine, and we packed no picnic baskets. It was a holiday that left a hole in time itself. "If you know of a better 'ole, 'op to it." I know, for I was there, in it up to the neck.

It all happened almost overnight. Men who had gone to bed, proud of the ornate buildings they had built, became their own janitors in the morning and carried out the garbage. Even the gar-bage job petered out when the rent-free tenants ceased to accumu-late it. Women who had worn pearls at breakfast rolled up their sleeves at lunchtime and handled the frying pan. Mrs. Allen C. Mason, in her castle in Mason's Addition, held her head high above the thousand-dollar India shawl that she had acquired on her mem-orable trip to the Orient, but she shivered at the same time, lacking fuel for the oil stove. Rattling streetcars ran empty while they jingled importunate bells, for men who had driven to the office in grand carriages now had no nickels to spare from the demands of the stomach. An owner would stoke the furnace of his half-completed building, while the financier who held a third mortgage on it wore the dreary hours away in the elevator, ready to pull the rope and lift some once wealthy down-and-outer to the third story. "There were giants in the earth in those days," inconspicuous giants of courage, husbanding their worn-out tools against the day of reconstruction. The remittance man, the outcast with the steady income hitherto had been the butt of the town wag. Now he came into his own, followed about by the jokesters of yesterday in the hope that a dollar might be forthcoming; and if a dollar couldn't be extracted, a dime would help. The sheriff was busy with auctions. A judgment for seventy-five thousand dollars against a respected citizen was sold for seventy-five dollars — and at that, the money of the unlucky bidder went down the drain.

Building stopped as though the whistle of eternity had blown. Pacific Avenue, so lately the home of bustle and hum, slept.

I tramped the plank sidewalks for orders. All I got was the orders for a wheelbarrow load of number three boards with which to board up the windows of deserted houses. The Tourist Hotel was my last hope. Surely the Northern Pacific would not let Tacoma down — Tacoma, the child of its loins. I found Mr. Goss, the contractor, in his office shack, gazing dejectedly at the yellow brick walls, still unroofed. His face was a map of despair.

"Young feller," he said, "the Northern Pacific's gone into the hands of a receiver. It's the fault of those damned Wall Street fellers. There ain't going to be any hotel."

No trick in the whole book of salesmanship could wheedle an order out of a dead project. Down the hill to the office I went, to bring the news to George Osgood.

George beat me to it. He hitched himself onto a high stool. "Our bank busted this morning," he said.

I hitched myself up to another stool. We looked at each other and laughed as though nothing so funny had ever happened before. Good old George, he was always ready with a laugh in time of crisis.

"I drew out our whole balance yesterday," said George. "Two hundred and sixty-seven dollars."

"Let me feel it. Nobody is broke who has two hundred and sixty-seven dollars."

I loaded my pocket with the gold and silver and fared forth to the Pacific National Bank. Mr. Manning greeted me with a sympathetic grin.

"Among the mourners this morning?"

"Mr. Manning," I said, "We've got to find a new banking home."

"Welcome," said Mr. Manning. "How much have you got?"

"Two hundred and sixty-seven dollars."

"Check or cash?"

"Cash!" I emptied my pockets.

"Masterson!" he called, "Tom wants to open an account."

"And now," I said, "we shall need a little line of credit."

Manning's face fell. "How much?" he asked.

"Oh, about ten thousand dollars," I replied.

A banking problem was presented: how much would two hundred and sixty-seven dollars in cash weigh against a deferred liability of ten thousand dollars? The cash outweighed the liability: I got the credit. Disaster was postponed, the next payroll was secure, and I could draw my salary. In truth, I had earned it.

And in truth, I needed it, for my first-born, Clem, selected that bright time to be born into an exciting world. Excitement was ever Clem's business, and he began it under the ministrations of old Doctor Munson and a pretty little nurse who was called in for her very first baby case. Doctor Munson didn't believe in anesthetics. "Opiates," he called them, "to block Nature's purposes." But he was handy with the forceps. For a horrid day and night, Charlotte obeyed the good doctor's injunction to "push — and help yerself," till at last he reached for his forceps. The little nurse stood by, her eyes bulging out of her head. She said she had never seen anything like that before. I thought she was going to faint. (She confided to me later that she had thought so, too.)

Clem arrived, terribly tangled up in his lifeline; the breath of life was spanked into his tiny body and he howled his protests. I was allowed to carry him into the bedroom and introduce him to his mother. Charlotte looked, her maternal delight a trifle dampened. "You little Siwash!" she said.

Clem grew up to write books, short stories, long stories, and motion picture scripts. If only he could stretch his memory to that day of his arrival into an economic vacuum, he would have a fit subject for an exciting story, for drama is Clem's business.

Unlike me, Brother Will had spent the four years of his education at Massachusetts Institute of Technology getting discipline, developing character, and acquiring a proficiency in mechanical engineering with which to face his world. Unlike me, he graduated with honors, almost too tired to face the life he was preparing for. In Tacoma he was growing more tired of the struggle against odds. He came home from the factory at night, jaded in all but determination, to sit in his easy chair, gathering strength for his next day's battle with power transmission, pulleys, belts, and suchlike things, all whirling to no apparent purpose, for no one seemed to want the product of all that power.

Then a telegram came to tell us that our younger brother Ned was dangerously ill. Ned was the baby of the family, on whom we all depended to carry on the Vermont tradition. Rutland, the little white house, without a Ripley there? It was unthinkable. Will packed his bag and left for Vermont.

Ned died, and the long journey, the anxious days of watching, and Father's grief all took a heavy toll of Will. He was taken to the Saranac tuberculosis hospital, then to Denver, and from there to Estes Park, high in the clear air of the Colorado mountains. There I joined the stricken family, taking Will's wife Belle and their three children.

In Estes Park I slept in a tent. The tent lacked a mirror, but I found one. Mother, with a shamefaced apology for her Vermont superstition, begged me to take great care not to let the mirror be broken. To reassure her, I sewed the mirror to my tent wall with heavy twine, strong enough to hold a hundred mirrors, and called Mother to look. "We take no chances," I said, and we laughed at the old fear that had bedeviled our New England forebears. That night a mountain storm let loose its fury against my tent; the mirror banged against the canvas wall and was smashed into a thousand bits. Will died the next day.

Within the space of a few months, Father's two workers had gone, leaving him only his fiddler-son to carry on. We carried Will down the rocky road to the railway for the trip to Denver, where we boarded the eastbound train for Vermont. I lay awake in my berth, listening to the clicking of the car wheels as they beat out the refrain of the lugubrious song of the day, "In the Baggage Coach Ahead."

In Rutland Will's coffin was carried through Merchant's Row, back to the house with green blinds. All that could be done was done; all that could be said was said. We left him with Ned in Pine Hill Cemetery. Father, his rugged exterior no longer able to conceal

105

the tenderness that lay underneath, did a strange thing for a Vermonter of his breed as we left the white house with green blinds. Dropping his mask for the instant, he went to the foot of the stairs and called up to the vacant rooms, "Will? Ned?"

His heart strained to listen. Then he turned, locked the front door, and with Mother walked for the last time down the marble walk to the gate. He didn't look back.

CHAPTER XVIII

CLOSING THE GREEN BLINDS on the white house in Rutland was like erecting a barrier between a past which was all rosy light and a future which looked murkily dark. I looked out over the green croquet lawn where we boys had fought over our games and, on the other side of the marble walk, at the sunken area which had served as our skating rink. I walked around to the east side of the house, where we had swung gloriously on trapeze and rings and to the big barn, still haunted by the spirit of my pony, who had long since gone to horse heaven. The green-clad arms of the elms, reaching skyward, reminded me of the span of comfortable years that lay behind me and made the children who had played under them look, in retrospect, so tiny. I thought ruefully of the spindling little Vermont elms that I had carried to be transplanted in a strange environment in front of Will's house in Tacoma. I cannot efface the memory of that moment, nor do I wish to.

Father, though his grief and his years weighed heavily upon him, squared his shoulders to the years ahead. He repeated, "There's work for you to do, son."

And, as before, I repeated, "Yes, sir."

I went to New York to try my wings as a salesman in a big way. Weren't we destined to "reach out and lead"? We must ship our carloads of lumber products from Tacoma to the eastern seaboard. I knew nothing of the pattern of big business: jobbers who bought carloads and distributed to retailers who, in turn, sold to builders who sold to house-owners. I didn't even know there were such things as jobbers, jealous of their rights to the trade of the retailers and so on down the line. In New York I studied the big city directory for names of dealers and walked out from the old Grand Union Hotel in search of trade. I presented myself at all the little lumber yards listed in the book. It was a weary job. I got here a pitying smile and there some brusque treatment but no promising welcome anywhere.

107

"Tacoma? Where's that? Cedar doors? Never heard of 'em." In all New York there was no lift to my spirit.

I went to Boston by the Fall River Line. It was cheaper. Walking the deck as we rolled around Point Judith, I counted on my fingers the blows I had taken on the chin during the year. I hadn't fingers enough, and my chin was pretty sore. I wore an opal stickpin in my tie. I pried the opal from its setting and threw it overboard. It was a constructive act of superstition and I felt better. Lightened of that omen of bad luck, I came to Boston where, at least, there were Yankees of familiar speech to deal with.

And, on Haymarket Square in Boston, without the opal stickpin, I found a jobber, the first of his breed that I had encountered. He was tough Yankee, but he listened as one Yankee to another.

"We buy our doors in Maine," he said, "pine doors. Grandfather used pine doors, and I guess what grandfather used is good enough for Boston." And then, the Yankee coming to the surface, "What's the price of these cedar doors, anyway?" he inquired.

And did I make the price low!

"Well, that makes a difference, of course." He hitched his chair up closer and told me what I must do. "You gotta educate the public," he said. "You gotta go to the house-owners and make 'em *like* cedar doors. Then they'll go to the builders and the builders'll go to the retailers an' the retailers'll come to me. See?" He beamed with the simplicity of his plan.

How this succession of buyers were to fall in love with a wood they had never heard of, from a place on the map three thousand miles away, was my problem to solve. I was just young enough and just verdant enough to tackle it. North to St. Johnsbury, down east to Portland I went. I swung around the traveling man's circle: to Worcester, Danielson, Norwich; on to Providence, Pawtucket, Attleboro, where they made jewelry; Woonsocket, where, according to the geography book, they made thread; and back to the old South Station in Boston.

I must have become a legend like the Wandering Jew. A friend, traveling on the New Haven Railroad, overheard a fellow passenger say to his neighbor, "Whaddaya know! There's a young fellow rattling around New England, trying to sell doors, made out o' *cedar*, from way out in Tacoma, state o' Washington!"

In Fall River, Massachusetts, one of the stops on my route, lived my old classmate, the Reverend J. Franklin Carter, ministering to his first parish. I loved to spend an evening with Johnnie, for he fairly exuded comfort and courage. Besides, Johnnie was a house-owner, and, what was more, one of his parishioners was a builder. The two of them introduced me to a third link in the chain, another of Johnnie's parishioners who also parted his name on the side — one A. Homer Skinner, who ran a lumber yard. Thus was the value of a college education demonstrated, and all the links in the chain of merchandising forged. Through my classmate Johnnie I got my foot inside the door of business.

A. Homer Skinner's name belied his nature; he was not a skinner, but a true Yankee, intent on buying cheap and selling dear. My price was cheap; so he bought the very first carload of doors to travel from the Pacific to the Atlantic. And, as that first freight car carrying cedar doors rumbled over the mountains on its way east, it passed the last carload of pine doors going from the Atlantic Coast to Puget Sound. The shift was as sudden as that.

I find romance in that story. To any fellow who recognizes romance when he sees it, there is plenty of it in the modern business world. To one who has bade goodbye to romance I say, "Don't go into business." Let him take up the law and feed his soul on torts and suchlike things.

With my precious order in my pocket, I almost ran to the station, lest Mr. Skinner change his mind before the train could take me away. Tingling with the sense of accomplishment, I waited on the platform. A carload of doors! A thousand of them! Would the trade ever exhaust such an inordinate number of doors? I doubted it. I couldn't project my imagination to a future when ten carloads at a clip would be all in the day's work.

I went back to Tacoma, stopping off in Chicago and going the rounds of the lumber jobbers, a huge joke to the big shots of the lumber trade, who bought their doors in Oshkosh. But the little seed I sowed took root later.

Puget Sound was about the deadest place in a moribund country when I emerged from the western portal of Nelson Bennett's Stampede Tunnel and coasted down to the depressed-looking old station in Tacoma. Self-contained Vermont, living contentedly on the produce of her narrow valleys, was far indeed from this scene of hope blasted by economic processes over which we had no control.

Our company was counted upon to fail. Why not? Failures were very fashionable. As the song of the day went, "Everybody's doin' it — doin' it — doin' it." An enthusiastic brakeman on the nine-thirty train, secure in his own job for the moment and all hopped up over a new tidbit of failure, jumped from his caboose at Puyallup and shouted, "Wheeler an' Osgood's busted!" Before noon every creditor in the valley came to pay his morning call.

Mr. Wheeler met them with the air of a man whose rich uncle had just died. He flashed A. Homer Skinner's order. "Doing a large wholesale business now," he said, "a carload business. Here's Mr. Ripley, just back from the East. Tell 'em about it, Tom." His confidence was infectious; it spread to the creditors. Again we had a reprieve; we bought new lumber for the new order on new credit.

CHAPTER XIX

ANOTHER NEW YEAR'S DAY dawned over our stricken town. The *Ledger*, its head bloody, but unbowed, greeted the day with its annual message:

Most of the people of the world have bidden good-by to the old year without regret. It has been a hard, cruel, cold, unproductive, and unhappy year. There has been no increase in it. Enterprise has been denied its opportunity, thrift its reward, and honest industry has, too often, been compelled to go both idle and hungry. The demagogue, the dead-beat and the Populist have alone survived. It may be that when the world shall have given up the hopeless effort to make the law provide for us all, and that when statesmen shall have worn themselves out and ground themselves to dust trying to make an elastic currency so elastic that there will always be enough in good times and a little more than enough in hard times, that people will cease to wait to be taken care of by legislation and, themselves, become so elastic as to readily adjust themselves to whatever happens. Quite likely hard times are made to give people a hint to manage their affairs more prudently. It is hard to see what else they are made for.

What the New Year may have in store for us, of course no man can tell. Those that have got through the past year may well look at it with hope and confidence. A story is told of an old Kansas farmer who was about to die. Friends thought that some spiritual provision should be made for the long journey he was about to make. They sent for the pastor of a neighboring church. The good man came and, after talking with the old gentleman for a while and finding him fully aware of his condition, asked him if it was not about time to make some provision for his future state. "No," said he, wearily and calmly. "It won't be worse than Kansas."

So, of the new year, it can't be worse than the two years that have preceded it, and as the present Democratic Congress must adjourn forever two months hence, it may be a great deal better.

111

I applauded that last phrase and took heart. I needed a stout heart, for the dreaded inventory was upon us.

Mr. Wheeler had his own notions about taking inventory and making up his annual report. All we had to do, said Mr. Wheeler, was to find, somewhere about the plant and the office, that seventy thousand dollars of paid-in capital that the books showed, and so come out, at least, even. His way was to add up the cost of the plant, plus the few dollars in the bank, plus the accounts receivable — all pretty bad or doubtful — and then deduct the account payable that couldn't be scaled down. The awful gap between the total and the seventy thousand must be found in the inventory.

"Go and find it," said Mr. Wheeler. "Depreciation? That's nonsense. There isn't any depreciation to write off. We keep this plant all mended up as we go along."

So we went after the inventory, looking at each item with a magnifying glass. We counted every stick of lumber, good or bad, every discarded monkey wrench, and all the odd nails that Mr. Osgood had picked up about the yard. It was a hopeless hunt for lost treasure. In spite of Mr. Wheeler's wholesome self-deception (and I'm sure it was wholesome, for we lived on it during those years), our capital of seventy thousand dollars had shrunk to twenty thousand.

"That's not so bad," said Mr. Wheeler. "We're not broke yet."

I told him he was an optimist.

"Yes," said Mr. Wheeler, "and you won't find any optimists in the poorhouse."

In Vermont we used to have a saying, "It pays to keep a-wigglin'," and I maintain that for those who keep a-wigglin', the age of miracles is not past. We had filed our sorry statement when a miracle occurred for us. A cheerful gentleman, fresh from South Africa, appeared in the office. He said he wanted to buy some doors. How many? He didn't rightly know; he had never bought any doors before. How many would I suggest?

They needed a lot of doors down there. He had, he said, a kind of a concession from Oom Paul Kruger, benevolent old Boer dictator down in the Transvaal, and a blank check. "Sight draft with the bill of lading," he said. I hadn't used that phrase before and it sounded impressive. He didn't quite know what sizes to order. Perhaps we could help him make up an order. Certainly we could. I helped him, generously. As orders have gone in later years, it was not so overwhelming, but to our famished eyes, it was like copious manna from heaven. Foreign money! Another payroll provided for! Maybe even a little left from which I might draw my own salary.

I fixed the gentleman up with a whopping big order. I introduced him at the bank, where his letter of credit was examined as though it was a curious historical document. I took him for a ride and gave him a lunch at the Tacoma Hotel, which cost a dollar.

"That's the stuff," said Henry Hewitt when I showed him the order. "It's what you sell *out* of a town that makes money for it. Swappin' real estate won't do it." I felt that I had received the accolade from a master town-builder.

Lunching at the Tacoma Hotel was a rare treat, not often afforded. Down in the south end of town, where substantial buildings later usurped the land, stood Sullivan's eating joint. If you passed your hand over the board counter, it came away all sticky with pitch. At Sullivan's, if you had two bits in your pocket, you could hitch up to the bar and get a luscious steak, dripping its gravy over a mound of mashed potatoes, a wedge of apple pie, and coffee in a massive cup. Sullivan's ribald cheer was thrown in. If a show-off had left a dime on the counter for a tip, Sullivan would have thrown it back at him. Outside on the plank sidewalk, there was always a friend or two who lacked the two bits, watching as you went in. A nod and a "good morning" meant "nothing doing." An incautious "how's things?" was followed by a firm finger thrust into your buttonhole, to hang there till the invitation was forthcoming.

Sullivan's was a good place. The price suited my pocket, the menu exactly fitted the vacant place in my stomach, and the company was always exhilarating. My heart was with Sullivan's, but as a man of affairs I sometimes frequented Knabel's restaurant upon Pacific Avenue. At Knabel's you ordered from a menu card, though you generally got something that resembled goulash.

At lunchtime the ex-millionaires gathered at Knabel's to talk matters over. The group came to be known as the Millionaire's Club, a club with no officers, no house rules, and no dues. Gathered about the round table, the community of the busted swapped stories of losses and made plans for recuperation. No club with marble columns and leather chairs ever housed a more genial membership.

Within the circle a select knot called itself the "Strategy Board," charging itself with the job of putting Humpty Dumpty together again. Billy Burrell sat in on the Strategy Board. He had his remedy: "Too many people in this town, walking about to save funeral expenses. What this man's town needs is about a thousand good funerals."

"Death rate's pretty high already," said Stuart Rice, "what with suicides and all. No. What this town needs is a thousand young men coming in, each with ten thousand dollars — and no experience."

Henry Hewitt repeated his standard maxim about selling out of town and added, "Most of you fellows came here with ten thousand dollars and no experience. Well, now you've got the experience."

George Hazard, his mind intent on the need of the moment, edged in on his crutches. Picking the most promising prospect for a touch, he squeezed in by Charlie Reeves. "Charlie," he said, "I've left my glasses up at Kachlein's to be fixed. I can't see anything without my glasses, and Kachlein wants three dollars for fixing them. Could you . . .?"

"Hell no," said Charlie. "There isn't anything in this town worth three dollars to see."

CHAPTER XX

THE NEAR-PARALYSIS OF Allen C. Mason's house-building empire ran its course to complete prostration. With the collapse of the boom in Tacoma, the tide of travel was reversed. Before the crash, the Northern Pacific trains had been loaded to the platforms with expectant travelers bound for Puget Sound. Now, the westbound flood turned to an eastbound trickle — a trickle of those who had the requisite political or economic pull to wangle a free pass, and to get a pass one needed only a shadow of influence. Those who couldn't cast a significant shadow and hadn't saved the price of a ticket stayed on perforce. There had been a popular song in the earlier days, the ballad of the Old Settler who, with his blanket rolled about his grub, prospected about the country in search of gold until he landed on the shores of Puget Sound. Some verses of the song still sing themselves to me as I write:

> I tried to get out of the country,
> But poverty forced me to stay
> Until I became an old settler,
> Then nothing could drive me away.
> No longer the slave of ambition,
> I laugh at the world and its shams
> As I think of my pleasant condition,
> Surrounded by acres of clams.

I am tempted to quote the whole song, a round dozen verses, for it so aptly suggests the role of the humble clam in the rebuilding of our town. We were surrounded by acres of clams, from the tide flats at the head of the bay, around Point Defiance, and down the Narrows to Olympia. The dispossessed, with the singleness of purpose that is stimulated by appetite, gathered at the beaches. Good company could always be found among fellow diggers, all intent on the little spurting sign that told where the clam lurked.

115

On the beaches there was always plenty of driftwood to be had, like the clams, without price. We quickly learned the trick of the clambake — the underlayer of dry wood, the seaweed, the clams, and then more seaweed. The long summer twilight was lighted up by the fires of the clambakers, and it was a heartening sight. What would have happened to the dwindling population of Tacoma without clams, I don't know.

Housewives vied with each other to invent new ways in which to set forth a feast of clams. Raw clams took first place, for they required no outlay for fuel, but we had steamed clams, roast clams, clams *au naturel*, and clams camouflaged. Although little clams were our first choice, we also dug the big "goeduc"— an obscene looking member of the clam family, tough and leathery, but good for clam broth. I was a guest at one dinner at which there were no less than twelve courses of clams, all bearing different names.

Knabel's restaurant, where the Millionaire's Club gathered, had clams at the top of its menu. Matt Meeker, the *arbiter elegantiarum* of our town whose social status, though he lived in a tent on the prairie, decreed that it was the duty of a gentleman to dine once a year at least *like* a gentleman, with a champagne bucket at his side, seated himself for his annual gorge.

"Bring me first," he said, "a dozen clams — and, waiter, please mention my name to the chef."

Ike Striker, playing with his toothpicks at a neighboring table, looked up. "Waiter," he called, "bring me a dozen clams — and, waiter, please mention my name to every damned clam."

Another dinner I had was wholly unlike the run of dinners at that time. It was a clamless dinner, but furnished through the agency of clams nonetheless.

Down under the footbridge leading to the factory, a flotilla of tiny houseboats jostled each other and rubbed noses as the tide rose and fell. There lived the happiest householders of our town, without benefit or restraint of law, and the tribe increased as the depression deepened. Among them lived a dirty old blighter, Mike by name, who dug clams for his living and peddled them to such householders on Nob Hill as had the price but not the initiative to dig for themselves. Mike sported an iron hook where his right hand once had been. He had a beard that spread fanwise over the area where his shirt front and tie should have been, a catch-all for whatever odd-

116

ment stuck to it — among other things, a tin tag or two that had caught there from his plugs of chewing tobacco. Mike was an economic royalist, abstracting his raw materials, free, from God's own pantry and selling them for whatever the traffic would bear. I felt a natural kinship with him.

Mike hailed me one day as I picked my way over the teetering planks, "Will ye come to dinner wid me? I got slathers o' food."

I joined him at noon and found him stirring a pot of what he called "th' eatin'est grub ye ever et." There was a pot roast, bobbing about amid carrots, onions, and potatoes. Mike grinned wickedly as he told me how he came by the feast. He had been peddling his clams at the back doors of Nob Hill when he looked in at the kitchen of the Garden house, where he smelled "th' best goddam smell in th' world." There was no one in the kitchen, but on the stove a kettle bubbled and steamed. The incense was too much for Mike. With his one good hand he opened the gunny sack and dumped his clams; then he used his hook as a pot lifter and made his getaway. We had a royal feed, and as we feasted, we commiserated with the Garden family, staying their hunger with clams.

Our clams were immortalized in a speech before the House of Representatives by George Cushman, who as a boy used to brag that some day he would "speak in the halls of Congress." He told the House a few truths about our depression and how he had weathered it, and the House listened. He wound up his peroration: "When the tide was out, our table was set. Our stomachs rose and fell with the tide."

God's blessing to the poor was not confined to the beaches; it was manifested offshore also. At Andrew Foss's boathouse we could, for two bits, hire a boat and Andrew's tackle. Andrew's advice was thrown in. With a half hour's noiseless dipping of the oars and a minimum of fisherman's luck, we could capture salmon enough to feed all the families on our street. (Once I even hooked a seal, which had grabbed my salmon just as the salmon struck my phantom minnow. I was devoutly thankful when the seal escaped with my salmon and my broken leader.) If our stomachs yearned for food more than our hearts did for sport, there was always a fisherman pulling in at Andrew's dock with an oversupply of fish, glad to sell a ten-pound salmon for a dime. Today I would not pay even a cent a pound — I am fed up with salmon for the rest of my life.

In later years my old friends Andrew Foss and his wife found their way, via the pages of the *Saturday Evening Post*, to their riches in the Hall of Fame. The story carried a picture of the old boathouse, which, when I studied it, made time turn backward through some mysterious dimension of space-time — backward through the blurred years to the clear picture of my young self, casting off for an hour's fishing.

"They're runnin' close inshore today," Andrew was saying. "Sneak up on 'em along by the Old Town Mill."

CHAPTER XXI

A PUGET SOUND MIST drifts across my memory of the town in those days of the big depression, obscuring all memory of despair and then parting to reveal a sun-lit glimpse of the community of the busted, accepting without a yelp the beating we had taken for our collective lunacy. Hope deferred, yes, and again deferred, but I cannot remember that it made our hearts sick. We were very young or very dumb, and in the bright lexicon of youth we failed to find the word *fail*. It was God's mercy to the innocent that we skipped the word.

We clutched our nickels and walked to the office in the morning, and gathered at the Millionaire's Club at noon to debate about the repeal of the Silver Purchase Act, the Homestead Strike, or Eugene V. Debs' Pullman Strike. We aired our views on Sound Money, of which, alas, sound or unsound, we had so little. We had begun to realize at last that national problems were, in some mysterious and malign way, related to ours.

The administration of President Harrison had dragged its innocuous way to its close. The impeccable moral atmosphere of the White House was not enough. A strong man was needed. The Democrats found one who proved disappointingly strong for the politicians, and, aided by Republican turncoats whom we called mugwumps, they elected Grover Cleveland. It was a good, old-fashioned, nasty-hot campaign, and an even more fervent heat was turned on when, on the eve of election day, some Republicans smirched themselves by springing the story of an affair of Mr. Cleveland's that had resulted in an illegitimate child. The campaign managers were flabbergasted. What should they say now?

"Tell the truth," said the four-square Mr. Cleveland.

I have always thought that this human dereliction of Mr. Cleveland's and his forthright honesty about it won enough male votes to elect him. (There were no female votes anyway.) Ike Striker voted for him.

"I think," said Ike, who had heard much of the McKinley Bill, "I'll vote for that feller that slept with th' Halpin woman. I think his name is Tariff."

After the election Mr. Cleveland, hard, uncompromising, honest, and wise, announced, "It is a condition which confronts us." In the tide-rip of social and economic forces beyond his comprehension, Ike agreed wholeheartedly. "He's damn whistlin' it's a condition," he said.

Our own condition at Wheeler Osgood was threadbare with examination, but I set about to examine it again. Again it totaled up about like this: lumber piles dwindling and Father's last loan about exhausted; credit dwindling with the lumber piles; a crew of hardworking men putting in ten hours a day, using up the lumber to make things that nobody had the money to pay for; payday coming with frightful regularity; men coming for their wages to an all but empty till and leaving us in the office looking hungrily at what was left for our salaries. I walked the planks over the Wheeler Osgood waterway, neglecting the theory but again pondering the condition.

It was lunchtime and I was hungry. Should I go to Sullivan's and eat, belly to the bar, or to the Millionaire's Club at Knabel's and sit at a table covered with a mangy-looking tablecloth and perhaps find a bit of comfort and inspiration? At Knabel's I found both. Mr. Mason stood outside, studying the menu pasted on the window.

"Liver," said Mr. Mason, "has risen in the social scale from the status of cat food to a place on the gentleman's table. Onions go with it. I shall dine on liver and like it." I chose liver, too.

Mr. Mason had inherited the traditions of one of his hellion ancestors of 1776. He had turned his hand to pretty much every occupation in the catalogue of the old-timers who had worked for their education, and in the process he had started many another ambitious fellow on the road to self-determination. I learned a lot, sitting at the feet of Mr. Mason.

We hitched up to the table at Knabel's and reached for the soda crackers. Soda crackers were free.

"Things looking up?" I asked hopefully. He knew and I knew that in the waste of shattered hopes, nothing was looking up, but how else was one to open up a conversation?

Mr. Mason munched a soda cracker. "Of course things are looking up," he said. "When you're flat on your back, there's no place to look but up. How's things in your business?"

"'Bout the same," I said. "Little more work with the bank to get a little more credit to pay a little more wages to get a little more food to get a little more strength to do a little more work; belt cinched up another hole and a few more hours at the desk, holding down the desk chair. Yes, I'm looking up, too."

We discussed the foreign situation with grave forebodings. The Venezuelan pot was boiling over. Mr. Cleveland was twisting the tail of the British lion over one of those everlasting boundary disputes, and it looked pretty ominous. We were not quite sure whether we were embarking on a war with Great Britain or were threatened with invasion by the Venezuelan Navy, steaming down through the Straits of Juan de Fuca to attack the City of Destiny.

There were disturbances aplenty in our own bailiwick, without going as far afield as Venezuela. As always, hungry and disillusioned men sought remedies for their troubles, and our town contained as big a proportion of hungry and disillusioned men as any town in the Union. Coxey's Army of the Unemployed was on the march, shouting its grievances as it marched, to lay them in the ample lap of President Cleveland. General Jumbo Cantwell, massive of frame and loud of mouth, clad in his new uniform of shining blue, led our town's threadbare, desperate contingent out to Puyallup, there to bivouac several hundred strong in a pre-empted vacant building. (I could hardly forget Jumbo. I had given him a wide berth in Harry Morgan's joint, where he had been chief bouncer.)

In Puyallup the Tacoma battalion sang their marching songs, and Jumbo made speeches, while they awaited the arrival of Seattle's contingent. From every crossroad town in the country the marchers gathered, moving in commandeered freight cars of railroads already in the hands of receivers, guarded by deputy marshals.

"The goddamn Northern Pacific got us out here," said Jumbo. "Now they're goddamn well going to haul us back."

Trouble was Jumbo Cantwell's business. He had found plenty of it when he and San José Bill kept rough order in Harry Morgan's saloon. He was a terror to all the fighting men of the county until he mixed with Eagle Eye Flannigan, the railroad detective, who found a holy joy in arresting him. I never knew how far the Washington state contingent got on their march to the national capital. Jumbo, with ranks thinning by desertion, rode the rails as far as

121

Chicago, where he eventually shouldered his way into the city council. I suppose his troops, when they quit, scattered as best they might.

Of course many schemes were proposed — large visions that added up to nothing at all — to pull us out of the morass by some miracle of social economics. Under other names, self-liquidating projects were devised, and share-the-wealth clubs were formed, with fancy names and fancy purposes. The Greedy Bankers, the Predatory Interests, and the Rapacious Merchants in turn took the rap, while all hands joined in singing "Damn, damn, damn the Northern Pacific!" And then, with denunciation still ringing in their ears, the businessmen quietly signed notes, without interest, to pay the interest on the city's bonds, which were about to default for lack of funds in the city treasury. In all the distress, I don't remember that anyone thought of calling on Washington for help.

Troubles multiplied with strikes on the railroad, strikes in the coal mines, strikes in every place where a little hell could be raised. Trains stopped running, and for days Tacoma was cut off from the outside world. Then, not content with the man-made convulsions, Nature took a hand. The Chinook wind blew up to bedevil us. The heavy snow on the mountain slopes turned to water under its warm breath and joined the torrential rains to swell the Puyallup River and maroon the city. Our green and lovely land became an island of desolation.

Blank despair was epitomized by Mrs. Melbourne Baily, who lost a silver dollar through the crack of the plank sidewalk and, overwhelmed by this culminating calamity, plumped herself down, feet in the gutter, and wept in the rain.

CHAPTER XXII

I HAVE NOT OVERDRAWN MY PICTURE of those days of depression on Puget Sound. Indeed, I feel that I have achieved a masterpiece of deft understatement. You simply can't overstate a vacuum.

We kept on living, and while we lived, we tasted the full savor of life. A letter from George Osgood many years afterward brought it all back to me. George was the fellow who first gave me his hand and his friendship when I blew into the Wheeler Osgood office so many years ago. He was, when he wrote the letter, still manufacturing doors and plywood on Puget Sound. He bemoaned the price of common labor:

> I think back to the gay nineties when a dollar and a half was good pay for a ten-hour day, and if there was anything left in the till for us in the office, we were in luck. Spuds were twenty-five cents for a fifty-pound sack; fifty pounds of flour cost forty-five cents, and two bits bought a fine thick porterhouse steak. Sometimes it was a choice between these luxuries and clams, but it seems to me we were more contented than we are now.

There was always some way to try circumventing what seemed to be inevitable disaster. The manager of the Tacoma Hotel, so lately and brilliantly opened, struggled valiantly to keep up the semblance of prosperity. He had a bright idea: "Sell Tacoma to the women-folks, and the men will follow." He began, quietly, to make it easy for young blades, who were stranded in town and who bore the brand of social experience to entertain young women at dinner. But the young women had to be the wives or daughters of visiting big shots from the East. Dinners, when a charming young woman was in town, were free.

"They come out here for fresh air and scenery," said the manager, "and we give 'em that free, too, don't we?"

Even big Captain Webber, headwaiter and steward, composed

his black face in a smile as he bowed the guests out, his hand empty of tips but his heart filled with pride of service, "All I get," said Webber, "is 'Much obliged to you.'" Other facilities of the town were free for the asking too: saddle horses from the livery stable across the street, little yachts and row boats anchored at the foot of the bluff, ready for a romantic sail. The young men about town became willing helpers in the job of popularizing the town with the ladies who represented the big money in the East.

The real estate subdivisions' business went into a state of suspended animation. The Kenilworth Addition was put on the market. It was named Kenilworth because its promoter had acquired the leftover stock of some publisher, a lot of handsomely bound volumes of Scott's novel. "Each and every purchaser of a lot in the Kenilworth Addition," said the hopeful promoter, "will receive, free, a handsome volume of this priceless literary gem, *Kenilworth*, by Sir Walter Scott. Come early and avoid the rush." The opening day dawned, but there was no rush and there were no takers.

The undismayed promoter grinned. "Tell you what we'll do," said he; "we'll do it this way. Each and every purchaser of a volume of Sir Walter Scott's *Kenilworth* will receive, absolutely free, a deed to a lot in Kenilworth's Addition." Again there were no takers. "Well, wouldn't that jar you!" he concluded and closed his shack office.

Perhaps a fellow might find an order or two for millwork in Everett. I took the old stern-wheeler *State of Washington* and went up to the newest city on the Sound, where a nail factory was planned, and where, it was said, whaleback barges like those on the Great Lakes were to be built to ply Puget Sound. I wallowed through the mud from the dock in a carryall, which, the driver said, was built so it couldn't tip over. It landed me on the other side of town, where a steamer, tied up in the Snohomish River, rented its cubbyhole staterooms to transient guests. For a week I picked my way about the place, wherever footing could be found in the sea of mud. I sailed back to Tacoma with an empty order book.

Spokane, now. No harm in trying; and you had to keep trying if you wanted to keep going. I wangled a pass on the Northern Pacific and took my first trip eastbound through the Stampede Tunnel.

The trip netted us exactly nothing. Spokane's Hotel Davenport was functioning, but only just. There was no business there, nothing to do but join the others who had nothing to do but look at the gold-

124

fish in the glass columns that held up the mantel shelf over the fireplace.

My cup ran over when I returned on the sleeper to find the "Italy of America" in the grip of a snowstorm, which had already laid a blanket a foot deep over the helpless town. No streetcars were running. I waded home in the early morning light to find all our water pipes frozen and Charlotte melting snow in a foot tub on the kitchen stove for water in which to wash Clem's diapers.

While we at the office were being dug out, we held a council of war and took account of stock: payday coming; notes coming due; a long list of accounts which couldn't be collected even with the aid of forceps, but which we continued to carry as assets, thus avoiding an item in red. We had no red ink and knew nothing of its use in the making of a balance sheet.

The word *boom* had disappeared from our vocabulary. While the population was melting before our eyes like snow before a Chinook wind, we talked bravely of "solid, substantial growth." But you couldn't make money on talk. If you had the money, you might take a flyer in Everett, up the Sound, where they were touching off a boom that might be all right — till it exploded. And there was Fairhaven, all blueprinted up — if you had the price. Seattle? Unh unh! A cultus lot of people and a cultus town, headed for the skids. Seattle, indeed! Trying to tag our mountain with the name of an unknown admiral — a British one at that. No, better stick to Tacoma. All together now; boost — don't knock!

We dramatized our situation with an eye to comedy rather than tragedy. We organized a select club and called it the Bluff Club. It was an appropriate name, both because we were natural bluffers and because our clubhouse was a hole in the bluff, down by the water's edge, its entrance guarded by a big boulder. There we stored a can of baked beans, some dried apples, and a hunk of ham. For obvious reasons, the club was a secret society — the secret of the cache closely guarded. We swore bloodcurdling oaths and adopted a motto: "One for all and all for one." We were all for the one can of beans and the one can of beans had, perforce, to be for all. The "club" was one of the many jests of the time, symptomatic of the lightheartedness with which youth faced its problems.

Harry Kissam, a young architect, was a most active member. Debonair, his pants creased from their night under the mattress, hat carefully brushed with his shiny elbows, the clean part of his handkerchief sticking jauntily from his breast pocket, Harry stood looking into the hopeful windows of Abe Gross's brick store. He twirled a malacca stick as I approached.

"Hello, Tom!"

"Hello, Harry! Where away today?"

"Well," said Harry, "I was thinking. I've just walked down the east side of C Street; and I thought I might walk up the west side this afternoon — not that I expect to see anything I haven't seen before. But you never can tell, Tom; you never can tell. Yesterday I saw my bank bust, right in my face. It was quite exciting. I thought if I walked down to the post office, I might get there in time to see that bust. But what about luncheon?" (Harry was a stickler for elegant English, so he said "luncheon.") "Do come down to the club with me, a quiet little place, and simple. You might call it a bit exclusive, as a gentleman's club should be. Do give me the pleasure." He twirled his stick and slipped his arm through mine with the hospitable gesture of the *bon vivant*. It was a regular rite, a little drama, staged just for the hell of it.

The horseless carriage had not appeared on our plank streets, and we developed the use of our legs on bicycles. A clear memory persists: Bill Seymour, who later became mayor of Tacoma, taking his girl to a party on a tandem bicycle, the girl's party petticoats pinned up in some miraculous fashion, Bill's dress tails caught up, out of reach of the mud, with safety pins. Bill was a Vermonter like me; and I suspect that, unlike me, he had the price of a Welch's Livery Stable hack; but he kept it put away for the rainy day that was now upon us.

"The longest, highest, and *only* bicycle bridge in the world" still carried us across Nick Delin's Gulch. Somewhere on the other side we built a golf and country club where we experimented with those newfangled golf clubs. The clubhouse was a board-and-batten shack in which could cut a slice of ham, put it between two slices of bread, and, with a bottle of beer, tell the world of champagne to go to hell.

All in all, our world of beer and sandwiches was a good world, and brave enough. Those were not unhappy times; and I like to think that in those days of adversity there was born the spirit that made Tacoma the lovely place of habitation and commerce that it is today.

126

PRINTED BY PENINSULA LITHOGRAPH COMPANY
TYPOGRAPHY BY SIBBERT TYPESETTING SERVICE
DESIGNED BY JOHN BEYER